S. HRG. 113–73

AMERICA'S CRUMBLING INFRASTRUCTURE AND HOW TO FIX IT

HEARING

BEFORE THE

JOINT ECONOMIC COMMITTEE CONGRESS OF THE UNITED STATES

ONE HUNDRED THIRTEENTH CONGRESS

FIRST SESSION

JULY 24, 2013

Printed for the use of the Joint Economic Committee

U.S. GOVERNMENT PRINTING OFFICE

82–357   WASHINGTON : 2013

For sale by the Superintendent of Documents, U.S. Government Printing Office
Internet: bookstore.gpo.gov   Phone: toll free (866) 512–1800; DC area (202) 512–1800
Fax: (202) 512–2104   Mail: Stop IDCC, Washington, DC 20402–0001

JOINT ECONOMIC COMMITTEE

[Created pursuant to Sec. 5(a) of Public Law 304, 79th Congress]

CONTENTS

AMERICA'S CRUMBLING INFRASTRUCTURE AND HOW TO FIX IT

WEDNESDAY, JULY 24, 2013

CONGRESS OF THE UNITED STATES,
JOINT ECONOMIC COMMITTEE,
Washington, DC.

The committee met, pursuant to call, at 9:55 a.m. in Room 628 of the Dirksen Senate Office Building, the Honorable Amy Klobuchar, Vice Chair, presiding.

Representatives present: Hanna, Maloney, and Delaney.

Senators present: Klobuchar, Casey, Warner, Murphy, Coats, and Wicker.

Staff present: Gabriel Adler, Corey Astill, Conor Carroll, Gail Cohen, Christina King, Connie Foster, Niles Godes, Colleen Healy, and Robert O'Quinn.

OPENING STATEMENT OF HON. AMY KLOBUCHAR, VICE CHAIR, A U.S. SENATOR FROM MINNESOTA

Vice Chair Klobuchar. Okay, we will call this hearing to order. We want to thank the Indian Affairs Committee. This is a beautiful room, and we hope to be back here. I really like it.

And we also want to thank our witnesses for being here to discuss the critical need to strengthen and improve our Nation's infrastructure system.

I am going to introduce first our distinguished panel of witnesses, and then say a few words.

We have Governor Ed Rendell, who was Governor of Pennsylvania from 2003 to 2011, and he previously served two terms as the Mayor of Philadelphia. He is Co-Chair and Co-Founder of Building America's Future, which focuses on the need for more significant investment in infrastructure in America.

Robert Poole is the Searle Freedom Trust Transportation Fellow and Director of Transportation Policy at the Reason Foundation. Mr. Poole, an MIT-trained engineer, has advised both Democratic and Republican administrations.

We also have Robert Puentes. He is a Senior Fellow with the Brookings Institution Metropolitan Policy Program where he also directs the program's Metropolitan Infrastructure Initiative. He is an expert on transportation and infrastructure, urban planning, growth management, suburban issues, and housing.

Chris Edwards is the Director of Tax Policy Studies at the Cato Institute. He is an expert on federal and state tax and budget issues. Mr. Edwards previously served as a senior economist with the Joint Economic Committee.

I think if we all look back at American history, we know how important infrastructure investment has been to this Nation.

We connected the East and the West Coasts by rail in 1869, which ushered in the Second Industrial Revolution.

We began building the interstate highway system in the 1950s. We did it with a Democratic Congress, I will note, and a Republican President.

And we are now at a state of need for infrastructure. I know that, coming from the State of Minnesota, where in the middle of a summer day, actually the anniversary coming up a few weeks from now, a bridge collapsed in the middle of my State. And as I said that day: A bridge shouldn't just fall down in the middle of America, not a bridge six blocks from my house, an eight-lane highway, a bridge that I drive my family over every single day. But that's what happened.

And as many of you know, we rebuilt that bridge with the help of the Federal Government in, literally in a year. I was just out there with our new Transportation Secretary, Secretary Foxx, out there on Monday, as one of his first visits. He also went to Connecticut to see where the train derailment had occurred just recently.

I think we all know this aging infrastructure does not suit our country. It is not America. And mostly, as we look at how we expand our economy so we become a country that makes stuff and invents things and exports to the world again, and we are in the course of doing that, to do that we need a transportation system that matches our needs.

That means not just highways and bridges, it also means rail; it also means, as a state that's on the Mississippi River, a lock and dam system that works to transport our agriculture products and other products.

So what we are going to talk about today are not just the problems—and we know there are problems—but it is also how we fix it. How do we get that funding mechanism that is going to get Democrat and Republican support? We certainly need bipartisan solutions to get this done.

The Senate has been acting. The Water Resources Development Act is a great example of that, which was a combined work of Senator Boxer, and Senator Vitter, and many others, including some of my colleagues here, where we were able to come together and reach an agreement. The bill is sitting over at the House right now, and I know they are working on it, but was an example of a piece of our infrastructure but certainly did not get to the level that we need at to get at the problems that we have.

Actually the idea for this hearing was Congressman Delaney's. I am going to give him a few minutes here to speak, and I would also note that my colleague, Senator Warner, is here, who has also been a big leader in infrastructure and we thank him for being here as well.

So I am going to give Congressman Delaney some of my time, and then we will turn it over to Senator Coats.

[The prepared statement of Senator Klobuchar appears in the Submissions for the Record on page 34.]

OPENING STATEMENT OF HON. JOHN K. DELANEY, A U.S. REPRESENTATIVE FROM MARYLAND

Representative Delaney. Thank you, Vice Chair Klobuchar, for organizing this hearing here today on this important topic. I want to also thank all of our witnesses for carving out the time to discuss this very important topic for our country and for all of their insights and expertise and commitment to this area.

As the Vice Chair said, we are all aware of the infrastructure challenges that this country has. The American Society of Civil Engineers estimates that we have almost a $4 trillion infrastructure hole as a country. And this is a very significant challenge, but it is also a very significant opportunity.

Because if we can in fact put in place smart infrastructure policy and design a prudent and efficient and effective way of funding the infrastructure in this country, we not only have an opportunity to put Americans to work in the short term, which should be a top priority of this Congress, but we also have an opportunity to improve long-term U.S. competitiveness.

And that is, to some extent, where the dimension of this infrastructure discussion is most important. As we think about competing in a world that is increasingly informed and shaped by globalization and technology, making sure we have an adequate, modern, and forward-looking infrastructure that's done in a smart way that allows U.S. corporations to compete is one of our central and, in my judgment, our most important domestic economic priority.

Because unless we compete successfully as a country, we will never be able to create jobs that have a good standard of living. And infrastructure is central to that discussion.

So I am very much looking forward to the panelists' comments today, not only on the needs we have as it relates to infrastructure but also talking about how we fund our infrastructure. Because I think there's a rich vein of support in this country for investing in our infrastructure, but there is significant debate and discussion about how we pay for that.

If you look macro at what is going on in the world today, you see this very significant infrastructure need which is typically a need that is provided by government, yet we look around and federal budgets, state budgets, local governments are strained.

So thinking about creative ways to finance our infrastructure that is fiscally appropriate in light of the larger fiscal challenges we are facing as a country is also part of the challenge. This is one of the reasons we have introduced the Partnership To Build America Act, which is a bipartisan bill in the House that invests in U.S. infrastructure, and ties it to tax incentives for the repatriation of overseas corporate earnings.

So with that, we'll get on with the hearing.

Vice Chair Klobuchar. Okay. Senator Coats.

OPENING STATEMENT OF HON. DANIEL COATS, A U.S. SENATOR FROM INDIANA

Senator Coats. Well thank you, Madam Chairman. I am standing in for Congressman Brady who could not be here, so it gives me an opportunity to make an opening statement, which I am going to ask unanimous consent to include in the record so that we can get to our witnesses.

Let me just make a couple of quick points here.

Vice Chair Klobuchar. Okay.

Senator Coats. It is clear that there is a consensus that infrastructure is crumbling all across America. Governor Rendell, Pennsylvania is one of the original Colonies, so you have some of the oldest infrastructure, but even as we work across the Midwest and into the West, we see falling bridges. We see crumbling infrastructure. We see pipes bursting underground. So clearly there is a consensus that we need to go forward and deal with this.

We all know that we are in this current fiscal dilemma of what comes first, almost a chicken-and-egg type of situation, where we know we need to spend upwards of a trillion and maybe even more dollars to address, over a period of time, to address this infrastructure problem.

We know that in doing so it potentially could provide some stimulus to the economy. However, we also realize that we simply are not liquid. We have to borrow funds in order to accomplish this. And in doing so, we then just fuel more debt, more deficit, which acquires more interest payments.

And when we put that together with the projected increase in entitlement spending with the retirement of the Baby Boom generation, we realize that the pot of money that falls into the discretionary category, that which we have authority over how to address, and where to spend it, and establish priorities, that continues to squeezed.

In fact, the projections are that in 10 years from now 90 percent of our tax revenue will be eaten up through interest and mandatory spending.

So no matter how earnest we are, and how committed we are to address a whole number of issues that fall in that discretionary category, not to mention health research, and not to mention education, not to mention any number of things that are priorities for Members of Congress, we have to understand the realities of the fiscal situation we are in.

So just a comment here relative to the fact that we do need to address this issue if we are going to go forward with a number of the plans that have been proposed, which have some real significance.

In my State of Indiana, we have had to, under a previous governor, and I think carried on by this governor, we have had to turn to public/private partnerships. That has been very successful for us. By leasing our toll road for a 75-year lease, we have been able to accomplish some very significant improvements in our transportation infrastructure.

These so-called P3s, Public/Private Partnerships, may be ways in which we can work around some of the fiscal limitations that we have. I might note, just from entering into that in just one area, through our toll road by the end of the year 2012 in Indiana we have completed 65 roadway projects; 19 others were accelerated.

We have completed 375 new centerline miles, 48 new or reconstructed interchanges, 5,030 preservation center line miles, accounting for 40 percent of the state's inventory, and rehabilitated or replaced 720 bridges.

So this may point a way into which we can address more immediately some of our infrastructure problems. I am anxious to hear from the panel, Madam Chairman, as to what their thoughts are on this and anything else they want to bring to us. So thank you, very much, for chairing this Committee and we look forward to the testimony of the witnesses.

[The prepared statement of Senator Coats appears in the Submissions for the Record on page 35.]

Vice Chair Klobuchar. Well thank you, very much. Thank you for being so brief. And I know that Senator Casey wanted to say a few words about Governor Rendell from his home State before we begin.

OPENING STATEMENT OF HON. ROBERT P. CASEY, JR., A U.S. SENATOR FROM PENNSYLVANIA

Senator Casey. Governor, you will be happy to hear me say that I am going to keep my comments brief.

[Laughter.]

But we have had a number of great governors of Pennsylvania. One of them was my father, and I certainly put him in certainly a special category, but we have had very few in the history of the Commonwealth that got as much done in four years, and then the second term for a total of eight years, as Ed Rendell. Remarkably effective Governor.

I will just mention, in addition to the focus on infrastructure and transportation and economic development, one part of his record, which will be an enduring legacy, is education—especially investment in early learning, which will pay dividends for several generations.

So we are honored that he is here to talk today about infrastructure, but I am especially grateful that my friend is here to watch how the Senate works at these hearings, and once in awhile we are all very brief, and today will be one of those days, Governor.

We are grateful you are here, as well as the other witnesses.

Vice Chair Klobuchar. And it looked like Senator Warner wanted to add something, as a fellow governor.

Senator Warner. I will simply add two quick points.

One was, I hope when Senator Coats mentioned that Governor Rendell was from one of the first Colonies that he didn't imply that Governor Rendell was one of the early Colonists, as well.

[Laughter.]

Vice Chair Klobuchar. I was thinking the same thing, but I didn't——

[Laughter.]

Senator Coats. Governor, that thought never crossed my mind.

[Laughter.]

Senator Warner. I would simply say that one of the things a number of us, and I really appreciate the Chair holding this hearing, is not only how we find that permanent source of funding, but how we also use tools—and this is something Governor Rendell has been working on—on how we create at a national level something that every other industrial nation in the world has: an infrastructure financing authority that allows us to centralize the financing, kind of intellectual capacity, to be able to kind of partner with Wall Street in a way the public sector gets protected to be able to put in place long-term debt, and to be able to have some form of that government backstop again that every other nation uses as a tool.

My hope is that we can find some consensus around this tool. It's not a full solution set, but it is clearly a tool we need in our toolbox, and I particularly thank Governor Rendell's work on that.

Thank you, Madam Chair.

Vice Chair Klobuchar. Okay. Well thank you very much, everyone, and I think we are ready to begin with the testimony. Governor Rendell.

STATEMENT OF HON. EDWARD G. RENDELL, CO-CHAIR, BUILDING AMERICA'S FUTURE, WASHINGTON, DC

Governor Rendell. It's a pleasure to be here, Madam Chairman, Senator Coats, Representative Delaney, of course Senator Casey, my good friend Senator Warner, and all of the Members of the Committee.

Thank you for holding this hearing. But I go to too many hearings on the question of infrastructure and transportation, and nothing significant gets done. Nothing significant gets done.

And that is different from what is going on in state capitals. It is different than the desires of the private sector. We want to get stuff done. We need the Federal Government to be a participant.

Congressman Delaney outlined the American Society of Civil Engineers' report. They do it every four years. They found that our infrastructure in general ranked at a D+. They found only six areas of improvement. And they were slight improvement: rail, roads, bridges, solid waste, drinking water and wastewater.

What do three of those things have in common? Over the last five years, states and the Stimulus bill invested significant dollars in rail with the TIGER (Transportation Investment Generating Economic Recovery) program, in bridges and roads, and improvements were made because of those investments.

We cannot be any clearer. In 2012, Building America's Future put out a report that was labeled "Falling Apart and Falling Behind," and we quoted the World Economic Forum which ranks the infrastructures of the world.

In 2005, the U.S. ranked first in the world for the economic competitiveness of our infrastructure. Now we rank 14th. We were 18th in rail, 19th in ports behind countries like Estonia and Iceland, and 30th in air transport behind Malaysia and Panama and many, many other countries.

It is a question of economic competitiveness. It is a question of economic survival. If we want to continue to be a first-rate economic power, if we want to protect our public, if we want to improve the quality of life of our citizens and our environment, if we want to create good, well-paying jobs that cannot be outsourced, it is time to do something. It is time to do something. What has been recommended? The American Society of Engineers—actually, Congressman Delaney said $4 trillion, over the next 8 years, the unaccounted for dollars come to $1.6 trillion. So they want to invest over $200 billion additional money a year in our infrastructure.

That is exactly the figure that BAF in its report recommended, $200 billion in additional spending over the next 10 years.

Your own Surface Transportation Reform Commission that the Congress authorized reported in 2008 that, just for transportation infrastructure you needed to spend at least $225 billion a year. And the CBO in 2010 said that an additional $185 billion annually spent on infrastructure—I recommend you read this report—would be justified by the economic and societal benefits it would bring to the United States of America.

If you look at these figures they are daunting and obviously Senator Coats set the environment that you have to deal with. My first suggestion is: Deal with it and find ways to reduce spending and increase revenue to fund something that is essential to this country's competitiveness going forward. Deal with it.

If we are making all of these spending cuts, and we are increasing revenue, let's find a way to fund something that will invest in our future and do something for the country. You cannot name me one American company that has grown successful that did not invest in its own growth.

We have got to invest, and we have got to start doing it now. And the good news is, you do not have to do it by yourself. That $200 billion figure does not all have to come from the Federal Government. It can come from the states. It can come from the private sector. The private sector in the U.S., and private sector abroad in places like China and Europe that have tens of billions of dollars that they're waiting to invest in a stable American infrastructure.

So let's look at where we are. Look at what the states have done. I am going to read you just a quick synopsis of states who in the last two years have passed revenue increases to deal with their infrastructure problems.

And, Senator Coats, states have to have a balanced budget. They have got more economic pressure than the Federal Government has. Listen to this array of states, because it is blue and it is red, it is Republican legislatures and Democratic legislatures. It is Republican governors and Democratic governors: Virginia, Maryland, Wyoming, Nebraska, Arkansas, South Carolina, Massachusetts, Texas, and Oklahoma.

And in Pennsylvania and Michigan, in two of the biggest states in the country, governors have proposed—Republican governors have proposed significant spending increases for transportation infrastructure. It is not blue or red, it is not Republican/Democrat. You know it's not Republican/Democrat. Senator Inhofe, arguably one of the most conservative Senators in the United States Senate, has said that infrastructure spending is the second most important thing we can do after defense spending.

I testified before Congressman Shuster's first hearing as Chairman in the House, and there were 50 of the 60 members present, and virtually every one of them spoke—albeit briefly—and almost every one of them pledged themselves to find a way to invest in infrastructure. There were Tea Party members, conservative Republicans who said I'm a Tea Party member but I believe we've got to spend money on our infrastructure. I'm a conservative Republican, but we've got to find a way to invest in our infrastructure.

Well, we can find a way. And there is no excuse for not doing it. Because the cost is high, Senator Coats? Of course is it high. The cost figures I have given you are almost astronomical, but one thing that Congress never computes is the cost of doing nothing.

Let me submit to you that the cost of doing nothing to the American economy and to the American consumer is greater than the cost of spending money, even at the level that I have recommended.

The United States Chamber of Commerce—not exactly a radical leftist-leaning organization—has estimated that each year business loses $1 trillion, the GDP loses $1 trillion that would be produced by having a first-rate transportation infrastructure. That is $1 trillion a year. Think of what a $10 trillion over the next 10 years increase in the GDP would do for your debt problem. Just think about that.

The Texas Transportation Institute says that the average consumer pays $818 a year in wasted time and additional fuel costs because of congestion on our roads. $818 a year. If you increase the federal gas tax by 20 cents a gallon, that would only cost the average consumer around $400. $818 to the average consumer.

So you are not alone in this fight. We can fund this together. The beauty of TIGER was the states competed. And an important part of TIGER grants was how much the states were willing to put up. They asked for federal money for the project, and often there was private money. Two of the most successful TIGER projects went through Pennsylvania and six other states. They were the National Gateway and the Crescent Corridor. One for CSX and one for Norfolk Southern, to increase our freight capacity in the Eastern half of the country.

The companies put up about 40 percent; the states put up about 35 percent, and the Federal Government through TIGER put up 25 percent. And because of that, our freight capacity in the Eastern half of the country is infinitely improved. We are going to be much more competitive because of that.

So you have got states willing to do it. You have got the private sector willing to do it. You have the people willing to do it. In every federal election, every election that's held on an even year since 2000, transportation referendums have been approved over 75 percent of the time, with the exception of 2010—arguably the most conservative election in our history or at least in our recent history and 61 percent of transportation referendums were approved even in 2010. And those referendums all called for increased borrowing, increased tolling, or increased taxes. And they were approved in blue states and in red states.

In South Carolina, two increases in the sales tax to fund transportation—one to rebuild the Port of Charleston because the residents of South Carolina knew how important the Port of Charleston was to their own economy.

So we can do this. BAF recommends that you take a number of specific steps—and I will run through these real quickly:

Number one obviously is find a way to continue funding TIGER. That competition for regional projects was—had a sensationally beneficial effect.

Number two, we've got to find a way, either through the TRIP (Transportation and Regional Infrastructure Project) Bond Program that Senator Wyden has proposed, or by bringing back Building America Bonds to aid the states in paying for their own investments in building their own infrastructure. The BABs program was an incredible catalyst for infrastructure development during the Stimulus. It was overlooked, but it was an incredible catalyst.

To generate private-sector involvement, we need to even expand the TIFIA (Transportation Infrastructure Finance and Innovation Act) Program more than you did in MAP–21 (Moving Ahead for Progress in the 21st Century Act). That was a great step in the right direction, but we would like to see it expanded even more.

Secondly, we think that we would either raise or eliminate the cap on Private Activity Bonds. That would generate a significant level of private investment.

Third, we've got to let the states toll interstates. In MAP–21, you allowed the states to toll interstates for additional capacity, but you did not allow us to toll interstates for existing roads.

If we are going to get the private sector involved, they need a reasonable return on their investment. And to do that, if we are going to maintain I–80 in Pennsylvania—Senator Casey is well aware of it—I applied to the Transportation Department for the authority to toll I–80. Right now, only the three pilot projects can be granted for tolling of previously accredited federal highways. I–80 cost us $200 million a year to maintain. $200 million a year just to maintain. It goes through the northern part of Pennsylvania which gets terrible weather.

We got turned down. We got turned down. But we were turned down because, the theory was, well why pay for it twice? The Federal Government paid to build the road. Why should we pay to maintain it?

Well that is like telling someone you pay to buy a car, but you don't have to pay to maintain the car. It makes absolutely no sense. The restriction on tolling federal highways should be lifted in the next transportation bill.

And last but not least, we need to create a national infrastructure bank as a catalyst for leveraging private investment, as it does in the very successful European Infrastructure Bank.

Senator Warner has a bill soon to be introduced. Congressman Delaney has a bill. Congresswoman DeLauro has a bill. They are all good bills in concept. It is very important that we get this bank moving, we get it funded with just a little bit of funding to catalyze the efforts of the infrastructure bank. It can be enormously successful, as the European Infrastructure Bank has been. The European Infrastructure Bank generates over $350 billion of investment in the EU's transportation systems, and not just transportation. And we can do the same.

I want to close by harking back to what Senator Klobuchar said in her opening. Eighty years ago the Public Works Administration bill was signed by President Roosevelt and passed by the Congress. That bill led to the building of the Triborough Bridge, the Lincoln Tunnel, the Grand Coulee Dam, the Overseas Highway bridge that linked Key West to the mainland of Florida. It sparked 34,000 transportation and infrastructure projects in the United States of America. It spent $6 billion, which would be the equivalent of $106 billion today, and it did wonders for the country.

We can do it. We can—Brookings just hosted a policy forum about the Can-Do States. If we had a Can-Do Federal Government that harkens back to all of the great times in this country's history when we faced challenges and met them by investing in our future, we could create millions, literally, 4 million new well-paying jobs that cannot be outsourced at the $200 billion level of investment. We can create millions of jobs. We can improve public safety, improve the quality of life, reduce the cost of doing nothing for our citizens, and return America to economic greatness.

So there are no excuses. The time to do it is now. The Simpson-Bowles Commission recommended doing something even in the midst of the debt restructuring. We can do this. We're Americans. We've done it in the past. We can do it again.

[The prepared statement of Governor Rendell appears in the Submissions for the Record on page 37.]

Vice Chair Klobuchar. Thank you very much, Governor. Mr. Poole, if our remaining witnesses keep it to five minutes, because I know there are a lot of people that want to ask questions, and thank you, Governor Rendell, for that great statement. Mr. Poole?

STATEMENT OF MR. ROBERT POOLE, SEARLE FREEDOM TRUST TRANSPORTATION FELLOW AND DIRECTOR OF TRANSPORTATION POLICY, REASON FOUNDATION, LOS ANGELES, CA

Mr. Poole. Thank you, Vice Chair Klobuchar and Members. I appreciate being asked to speak today.

My testimony, like the Governor's, will be limited to transportation infrastructure since that is my primary area of expertise.

Our transportation infrastructure is falling behind our global competitors in serious ways. Part of the reason is that our competitors make much greater use of long-term public/private partnerships for transportation infrastructure.

Today, nearly half of all air passengers in Europe are being served by privatized airports. And that trend began in 1987. We have privatized only one airport, San Juan International, and that was only just this year.

Over 50 countries have corporatized their air traffic control systems, giving them a bondable user fee revenue stream to make major capital investments, while our attempts to implement NextGen through the FAA are struggling, held hostage to federal budget problems.

In highways, much of Europe, Australia, Latin America, and even China are using long-term toll concessions to build their equivalent of our interstate highways, and we need to rebuild and modernize ours and do not have the money to do it.

A large majority of the world's seaports are either investor-owned outright or are using the landlord-port model in which the private sector builds and operates all the terminals.

Most inland waterways are government-owned, but some charge tolls, including the Panama Canal, which has issued toll revenue bonds to finance the $5 billion expansion that is going on. Meanwhile, our tax-funded waterways are plagued with obsolete and undersized facilities.

Now there is now a global infrastructure industry in transportation which can finance, build, operate, and maintain airports, highways, seaports, et cetera, but none of the major players are U.S. companies. We are missing out on this entire industry as a participant.

And of the $300 billion that has been raised over the past decade in infrastructure equity investment funds, while 30 percent of that money has come from U.S. investors, most of that money is being spent overseas because that is where the PPP opportunities are.

Now why does this matter? What are other countries getting by enabling large use of long-term PPPs in infrastructure? I see four major benefits.

First, as the Governor said, obviously more investment, which we desperately need, is important.

But I think even more important is more-productive investment. Because PPP projects, in order to be able to get financing, have to meet a market test. They have to demonstrate that the project's benefits will exceed the cost, and likely produce a return on investments. So that is a very important additional benefit.

Third, we can shift significant risks of infrastructure megaprojects from taxpayers to investors for risks of cost overruns, risk of late completion of the project, and risks of over-optimistic traffic and revenue projections.

And fourth, we can get guaranteed maintenance of the projects that are done by means of long-term PPPs, because the same entity that builds it does not just walk away, but is responsible for operating and maintaining it for a long period of time, as a business, competing for customers.

Now I think it is time to take a hard look at rethinking the 20th Century model the Federal Government has used for infrastructure, which is user taxes, trust funds, and grants.

It is not working very well. First of all, user taxes are now seen as just taxes, and any increase even though it would go for productive uses is seen as a tax increase and therefore very hard to get support for.

The model builds in a large amount of redistribution, and cross subsidy, which is not only inefficient but it also creates disaffection such as people believing the program is all about bridges to nowhere in Alaska.

Congress has created many unfunded mandates which using federal dollars increases the cost that states have to bear to build their projects. And the model encourages states to fund projects out of annual revenues rather than financing them over the long term, as all investor-owned infrastructure does: electric utilities, railroads, toll roads, and so forth.

The thrust of my written testimony is that it really is time to rethink the federal policy for the 21st Century in light of the government's ongoing stress. I think there are three key points for doing so:

First, we need to sort out which functions are truly federal in nature. Which transportation is truly federal? Refocus the Federal Government on that and delegate the rest to state and local governments where the need really is.

Second, shift from funding to financing, which means federal policy needs to begin shifting much more from grants to loans on a basis preferably that does not put federal taxpayers at risk. And a good example of what I like is Representative Delaney's American Infrastructure Fund, which would not put taxpayers at risk.

Third, enable states to take on a larger share of responsibility by removing tax and regulatory obstacles to enable them to make better use of long-term PPP. I suggest in my written testimony how this would play out for the different modes of transportation.

And I also provide a near-term list of tax and regulatory changes that could begin this transition, and a list of organizational changes, including corporatization of the Air Traffic Control System along the lines of the very successful Nav Canada, and enabling the Army Corps of Engineers to enter into long-term PPPs to replace obsolete locks and dams financed by toll revenues paid by those using the new facilities.

This is an ambitious agenda. I will wrap up by making just two points.

One, infrastructure is critically important to our economy. We need to do a much better job of funding and managing it. And the PPP approach could make a big difference in this.

The other is that, given the fiscal condition of the Federal Government, the 20th Century User Tax/Trust Fund/Federal Grant Money is unsustainable, and I think we really need to think hard about that.

That is the end of my testimony. I would be happy to answer questions when we get to that.

[The prepared statement of Mr. Poole appears in the Submissions for the Record on page 39.]

Vice Chair Klobuchar. Thank you, Mr. Poole.

Mr. Puentes.

STATEMENT OF MR. ROBERT PUENTES, SENIOR FELLOW, METROPOLITAN POLICY PROGRAM, BROOKINGS INSTITUTION, WASHINGTON, DC

Mr. Puentes. Thank you, Vice Chair Klobuchar, Members of the Committee. I very much appreciate the invitation to talk about this important topic.

I think the Governor and the members have already kind of laid out the need, and made the case for why we need to invest in infrastructure, so my remarks are going to focus on the ways the Federal Government can engage in new partnerships with both the private actors and the public sector to invest in infrastructure. And, by so doing, put Americans back to work and then rebalance the economy.

Today, low interest rates, coupled with the attention from private firms and foreign funds are presenting growing opportunities for a fresh set of focused, federal initiatives to support pragmatic public and private sector leaders in states and citizens and metropolitan areas as they collaborate and innovate around infrastructure investments.

So, for example, Congress should revive the Build America Bonds Program, as the Governor mentioned, to support state and local investments. Established in 2009, the two-year program authorized special taxable bonds with a direct federal subsidy that decreased borrowing costs and stabilized the municipal bond market.

Given the subsidy, they proved wildly popular, as the Governor noted. During their short existence, BABs financed one-third of new state and local long-term debt issuances. They were used in every single state, and for a variety of infrastructure, including educational facilities, and most notably for water and sewer projects.

In reviving BABs, lowering the tax subsidy from 35 to 28 percent would make the program revenue neutral relative to the estimated future federal tax expenditure for tax-exempt bonds.

Since states and municipalities do not really need the same aggressive subsidy they did after the financial crisis, I think that the lower rate really is appropriate for today's needs.

Next, while municipal bonds are geared toward infrastructure projects with a public benefit, private activity bonds are directed at those projects that primarily benefit private entities and also serve some public purpose, such as airports.

PABs are issued by state and local governments for projects with more than 10 percent of the proceeds benefitting a nongovernmental entity and are directly or indirectly paid back by a private business.

However, not being exempt from the Alternative Minimum Tax limits their ability to attract potential investors over time. Based on estimates from the Joint Committee on Taxation, eliminating the AMT on all PABs could potentially cost the government about $49 million annually over the next 5 years. Yet, the exemption would generate billions of dollars in additional economic activity and lead to cost savings of almost $750 million for airports alone over the next 10 years.

However, we know that Public/Private Partnerships are complicated contractual arrangements and they vary widely from project to project and from place to place. As the challenges to infrastructure development throughout the U.S. become more complex, there is a constant concern that public entities in some states, cities, and metro areas are ill-equipped to consider such deals and fully protect the public interest.

So one solution is the creation of a specialized institutional entity to assist with those expanding opportunities. These so-called PPP units would fill a variety of functions, including quality control, policy formulation and coordination, technical advice, and standardization.

These are voluntary and budget costs should be no more than about $3 million annually.

But another way to provide technical assistance and expertise to states and other public entities that cannot develop internal capacity to deal with the projects themselves is through the creation of a national infrastructure bank.

If designed and implemented appropriately, an infrastructure bank has the potential to leverage billions of dollars in private investment, as has been mentioned; provide a streamlined selection process for projects; and apply a more rigorous standard for evaluating critical investments.

14

A one-time repatriation tax holiday could be used to unlock the billions of dollars of domestically untaxed capital and finance the creation of the National Infrastructure Bank.

Today, American corporations hold over $1.5 trillion in domestically untaxed deferred dividend payments overseas. While similar repatriation holiday created for the 2004 American Jobs Creation Act failed to generate significant domestic stimulus, a targeted program focused on infrastructure has the potential to deliver job creating and economy building projects for decades to come.

By directing a percentage of the recovered taxes into the infrastructure bank, or else compelling corporations to invest a portion of repatriated funds into a special class of bonds that support the institution, Congress could encourage infrastructure investment here in this time of political gridlock.

Depending on the specific goals for the infrastructure bank, capitalizing it can occur in a flexible manner as well with levels ranging from $10 to $50 billion. Of course there are real costs, and there are real hazards associated with any repatriation-based program. However, policymakers must also weigh the concerns of those things against the strategic and financial benefits of a well-functioning strategic infrastructure bank.

Most of what I have described here will require legislative action, possibly as part of a major tax reform bill, or through budget negotiations, but I think we can do this.

Madam Vice Chairman, I know it will not be easy, but I think the time is right to invest in infrastructure projects that do put us on the path to a more productive and sustainable economy.

Thank you very much for the opportunity to appear before you today.

[The prepared statement of Mr. Puentes appears in the Submissions for the Record on page 45.]

Vice Chair Klobuchar. Thank you very much, Mr. Puentes. Mr. Edwards.

STATEMENT OF MR. CHRIS EDWARDS, DIRECTOR OF TAX POLICY STUDIES, Editor, *WWW.DOWNSIZINGGOVERNMENT.ORG*, CATO INSTITUTE, WASHINGTON, DC

Mr. Edwards. Thank you very much, Ms. Vice Chair, and Members of the Committee. Thanks for having me testify today.

Infrastructure is extremely important to the economy. We need to ensure that investments in infrastructure are as efficient as possible, and we can do that in my view by decentralizing the financing and ownership of infrastructure out of Washington as much as we can.

State and local governments and the private sector are more likely to make sound investment decisions without all the federal intervention we have today.

The first thing that's interesting to note is that most U.S. infrastructure is actually provided by the private sector. The private sector actually provides more than five times as much infrastructure to the U.S. economy as the federal, state, and local governments combined: pipelines, cellphone towers, you add it all up that is $2 trillion of private investment a year in infrastructure. Again, five times the size of government infrastructure.

So the policy upshot from my point of view, looking at that, is we need to also focus on things to increase private infrastructure investment such as doing tax reform.

That said, government infrastructure is of course very important to the economy, but I think it should be done as much as possible at the state and local level, not the federal level.

Why do I say that? A number of reasons.

Federal infrastructure investment is often misallocated, from my point of—from my opinion. Look at Amtrak investment, for example. In my view, a lot of it is based on sort of political demands and not based on actual customer marketplace demands.

Federal infrastructure is often not operated efficiently, is often not priced properly. So, for example, if you look at the Bureau of Reclamation's vast water infrastructure in the Western United States, it does not use market pricing. Water is vastly under-priced, which causes inefficiency.

Federal infrastructure is often mismanaged and has large cost overruns. The FAA has a very poor record in terms of bureaucratic mismanagement and cost overruns. And the key problem with federal intervention, it seems to me, in infrastructure is that the Federal Government when it steps it, it replicates mistakes across the country.

States and private companies make mistakes, but when the Federal Government makes mistakes it replicates it everywhere. The classic example of this is high-rise public housing, which everyone agrees now was a disaster, and was replicated in dozens of American cities in the mid-20th Century because of federal subsidies to cities to do this very inefficient infrastructure investment.

So those are the sorts of short-comings with government infrastructure that are one reason why there is growing interest in privatization in the United States and around the world.

I fully support P3s and partial privatization of infrastructure, and we should explore all those kinds of opportunities. But we should also look at full privatization where it is possible.

Airports can be fully privatized. London's Heathrow is a good example of that. Bridges can be fully privatized. There's a new $140 million Jordan bridge that was recently completed near Norfolk, Virginia, completely privately financed, owned and operated and constructed.

And Air Traffic Control, as Bob Poole has pointed out, has been privatized in Canada and Britain and other places. Indeed, I am really struck by the Canadian Air Traffic Control privatization back in 1996.

The Canadian Air Traffic Control System is a nonprofit corporation, separate from government. It does its own operations. It funds its own capital investments separate from government, and it has been an extremely successful model. It is one of the safest systems in the world.

You compare that to the FAA, the FAA has this big demand for funds. There's budget instability in Washington. The FAA does not know where it is going to get the funding. We saw with the sequester cuts that threatened to disrupt air traffic control in this country.

The solution, it seems to me, is to set up air traffic control as a separate nonprofit corporation like the Canadians have. So privatization and P3s have swept around the world, but not so much in the United States.

So why not? Well there have been a bunch of sort of built-in hurdles that Congress needs to look at that are preventing more privatization of P3s in the United States. A key one is that the Municipal Bond Tax Exemption favors public facilities over private facilities. That is a big barrier.

Canada, for example, does not have that barrier. Muni bonds in Canada are not tax-exempt and so private and public are on a more even keel.

Income and property taxation. If you want—if private entrepreneurs wanted to set up an airport, they would be taxed on their earnings. They would be—they would face property taxes. Government facilities don't pay income or property taxes.

And here is a key thing that people often overlook. Federal aid, or federal subsidies are often viewed as a positive, but there is a negative crowd-out effect of federal subsidies. And here's what I mean:

Before the 1960s, the vast majority of urban transit bus and rail in the United States was private. Bus systems and rail systems in cities across America were private. Then Congress passed the Urban Mass Transportation Act in 1964.

That Act gave transit subsidies only to government-owned systems at the local level. The effect by the end of the 1960s was that virtually all transit systems in America became public owned and we lost the competition and the innovation and entrepreneurs that private transit brought to America because of those federal subsidies.

So federal subsidies work against privatization at the state and local level.

There are other issues the Governor mentioned: interstate tolling requirements. I agree with him. We have to look at that. And there are other federal regulations that stand in the way of privatization.

So to sum up, you know there is widespread agreement obviously that America needs top-notch infrastructure to compete in the global economy. The way forward, in my view, is for the Federal Government to reduce its control over the Nation's infrastructure. State and local governments should be encouraged to innovate with privatization P3s to the fullest extent possible.

Let's get America's great entrepreneurs helping us solve our infrastructure challenges.

Thank you, very much.

[The prepared statement of Mr. Edwards appears in the Submissions for the Record on page 50.]

Vice Chair Klobuchar. Well thank you very much to all of you. I will get started here.

I note, Governor Rendell, you talked about the investment in Europe, the $350 billion that you mentioned, and you talked about the fact that they have a history of investment with public/private partnership. Could you describe what they are doing there, and how they got started in this way that allowed for more infrastructure, and what we can learn?

Governor Rendell. Well it got started similar to what Senator Warner and Congresswoman DeLauro want to do. The EU countries put money in to begin to capitalize the fund, and now the fund makes loans. It's exclusively loans. They make enough money on the repayment of those loans not only to cover their entire administrative costs, but to add money to the fund itself.

So it has been enormously successful.

Vice Chair Klobuchar. Is it an infrastructure bank, or is it a private/public——

Governor Rendell. It's an infrastructure bank that only loans monies to those projects where there's going to be a rate of return.

One thing I wanted to say to my folks from the CatoInstitute, I for a Democrat am probably the strongest advocate for public/private partnerships in the country, but let's not be deluded into thinking that private/public partnerships or privatization are going to solve all of our problems.

The country has 66,000 structurally deficient bridges, one of which was——

Vice Chair Klobuchar. Yes.

Governor Rendell [continuing]. Regrettably in Minnesota. Of those 66,000, my guess is no more than 1,500 could be tolled where there would be a reasonable enough rate of return to do the work necessary to rebuild or expand those bridges.

Some, yes. There is a bridge in Pennsylvania that is on I–95 going from New Jersey to Pennsylvania. It's not tolled now. If we tolled that bridge, we can expand from four lanes to six lanes with a side avenue for cars to go off. It would cut waiting time from 45 minutes in rush hour to 15 minutes in rush hour.

Vice Chair Klobuchar. Right.

Governor Rendell. We can afford to toll that. But the vast majority of bridges, the vast majority of roads, there's not going to be a private sector return on investment. Airports, yes. Locks and dams, perhaps. But there is some infrastructure that the government, whether it be state, local, or federal, is going to have to pay for.

Vice Chair Klobuchar. Right, and I appreciated your point that even the Simpson-Bowles report and that group, and the work that a lot of us have done in the middle on the budget, like Senator Warner, and others, we truly believe that you have to invest at the same time; that it is not exclusive. You can make that investment in some key things at the same time you're doing a long-term debt reduction by making some of the reforms that were talked about, and also looking at closing some of the loopholes and doing some other things.

Governor Rendell. And remember, when you're talking about federal investment, one of the problems with the way Congress scores is that there's never any offsets. That type of investment produces significant federal, new federal tax revenue by the jobs that are created, by the corporate profits, et cetera.

Where you start offsetting that, and offsetting the economic benefits, I again recommend your staffs to CBO 2010 report where the CBO—again, not exactly a leftist-leaning organization—says we can afford $185 billion annual increase in infrastructure investment because of the economic and societal benefits to us.

Vice Chair Klobuchar. Okay. Mr. Poole, Mr. Puentes, the infrastructure bank does actually include a version of it in the Build American Jobs Act that also had some increase—significant increase in investment on the government's side, and we got some support. We got a majority of the Senators, but I led that bill last year and we were not able to get it through the filibuster.

But could you talk about the infrastructure bank, how you see it working? And by the way, how would rural projects be included? I get that question a lot at home.

Mr. Poole. Rural projects I have not really looked into. That is a good question. I mean, you probably could not do the same kind of things that you could do in terms of robust revenues and things in more urbanized areas.

But infrastructure banks, I have been critical of most of the infrastructure bank proposals that have come along because I fear they do not have the same kind of protections that are built into TIFIA to ensure, to make it likely that these will be sound investments that have a dedicated revenue stream, and investment-grade bond ratings, and things like that.

That is why I draw a distinction between those and Congressman Delaney's new proposal that would not put the federal taxpayers at risk by creating debts that might not be repaid. And so I think we really need to be careful what we are doing.

I mean, it was one thing during the Depression——

Vice Chair Klobuchar. And this is tying it in with expatriation.

Mr. Poole. Yes. And that provides an initial capitalization that comes basically from the private sector, not from the Treasury.

Vice Chair Klobuchar. And I think, as Mr. Puentes pointed out, we tried this once and I think people are open to looking at it again, but the rate has to be right so it actually brings in the funding that we would need. And I think that's—and I know people in the Administration and others who are looking at it, but the rate is what—I think that will have to be determined to be the right point so we actually are bringing in significant money.

Mr. Puentes, did you want to comment further on that?

Mr. Puentes. Yes, thank you, Senator. I think that the members here are right. We have to be careful about this. An infrastructure bank is not a silver bullet. It is certainly not going to address all the challenges we have talked about here today. It is certainly not going to address all the things the Governor highlighted at the beginning, but we do see when we look around the room we see what the needs are in the United States.

And there is an omission right now, and we do not really have a way to make decisions on projects that are truly of national significance. So what we would like to see, what I would like to see, is some kind of entity that is focused on delivering the economic goals we have as a country.

So the President's goal to double exports in five years is exactly the kind of far-reaching, ambitious goal connected to the global economy that we have right now. An infrastructure bank that would kind of actualize some of those goals, there's obviously major freight projects that would come along with that.

Mr. Puentes. In and around the United States ports so that we are not investing in projects that are—are areas that are competing with one another.

Vice Chair Klobuchar. Right.

Mr. Puentes. And they would also address the rural areas. So freight moves all across this country. The country is very, very large and freight moves from Los Angeles, through Chicago, and elsewhere—obviously if you're a rural area, the rural areas would benefit from that directly.

Vice Chair Klobuchar. Right.

Mr. Puentes. So the infrastructure bank is not going to solve all challenges. I think that we are doing a good job on the transportation side, but I think that we also need something that is looking at clean energy; that is looking at other areas of infrastructure, water infrastructure, and not continuing the siloed nature in which we make infrastructure investments today.

Vice Chair Klobuchar. Yes.

Mr. Puentes. It is not going to solve every problem, but it is certainly going to fill a niche that we know that we need.

Vice Chair Klobuchar. Yes, and I think we have already seen that Congress was willing to come together on that last two-year transportation bill. Obviously a long-term bill is much better, but they are the seeds to get this done.

And I love your point about the goals, because I thought that was one of the best things the President put out there: exports doubling in a number of years. Because we are working to get to that goal, and it made a difference, and people remember that.

And so that kind of a goal with infrastructure tied in with some new ideas. And as the Governor pointed out, it is not a one-thing-fits-all. There was a guy, I was telling Representative Delaney, up in Moorhead and Fargo near Canada that actually is a guy that somehow got permission to be in a shack and charge 75 cents every time someone crosses the bridge. This is not good public policy.

[Laughter.]

And so that is not the one way to solve everything. And so I think it is a combination of things that you have talked about today, and I know there are people yearning to get this done, and I think it is one great thing we could do to bring people together. And basing it a lot—people don't talk enough about the freight issue, and the exports, and the industry willing to pay more for locks and dams. There are a bunch of people in the private sector that want to join in and be part of this, and we have got to give them the vehicle to do it.

All right, with that I am going to turn it over to Congressman Delaney while I go to Judiciary and hopefully come back, and Senator Coats, thank you.

Representative Delaney [presiding]. Senator Coats.

Senator Coats. Well this is an interesting topic here. I am enjoying the input that has been given us by the witnesses.

I want to go to an issue relative to what both Governor Rendell and Mr. Edwards were talking about, and that is the role of the Federal Government, the impact of keeping it within a political process.

You used the example, Mr. Edwards, of Amtrak. When the political process intervenes in the decisionmaking process, it distorts the market. And while Amtrak running up the East Coast is a demonstrated market, stops in your state, Governor, and yet in order to continue to subsidize that program—I am not going to name any particular states—but the line that runs from A to B better stop in Timbuktu to pick up the two passengers a month that get on there or I am not supporting anything that is going to stop in Philadelphia, or going up the Coast.

That is just a small example of what we run into. So I wonder, how do we address that? How do we pull all this—how do we define the federal role in a way that the politization process does not distort the market in a way that discourages investors from the private sector, in a way that misallocates money out of the taxpayer's pocketbook.

Any comments? I'll start with you, Governor, and then Mr. Edwards.

Governor Rendell. Let me start off with the fact that you have dealt successfully with one of the problems, and that is over-regulation of transportation infrastructure. MAP–21 did a very good job in reducing some of the regulations and cutting timelines.

The President, as you know, has issued an Executive Order to cut those timelines by 50 percent. That would be enormously helpful to us both on costs and in getting things done quickly.

So you have already done that. But the way to get politics out of the major projects, you are still going to have to give states basic grants to help them with their overall needs. But to take a good hunk of what the federal commitment is, give it to the infrastructure bank for projects of, as Mr. Puentes said, national significance and let states or groups of states, or private entities, come in and compete. And the infrastructure bank makes those decisions based on cost/benefit analysis, based on a review of the project to see whether they're workable, whether there's a reasonable return on the investment. That is one way of doing it.

A second way of doing it is through the TIGER grant process. The best thing about TIGER, one, it allowed states to combine an application. So we got regional projects.

Two, TIGER leveraged private investment.

And three, it was competitive. And the decision was made by U.S. DOT, and most of TIGER's decisions were based on cost/benefit, not on politics. Every state did not get a project out of TIGER. TIGER funded the major projects.

So the more competitive you make it, and the more you give the decisionmaking—I know Congress is always loathe to devolve decisionmaking to someone else, but if you give decisionmaking to people who are experts and who are somewhat insulated from the political process, we can do this. We can absolutely do it.

It works in Europe, and it can work here.

Senator Coats. Mr. Edwards, did you want to respond to that?

Mr. Edwards. You know, part of the idea with an infrastructure bank is to get more private financing for infrastructure, and that is great and I am all for that. But the problem with having a federal national infrastructure bank is that the decisionmaking on infrastructure projects becomes, you know, national and ultimately political decisions.

I can name you agency after agency, Army Corps of Engineers, on down the list, where politics intrudes decade after decade and you just cannot get around it at the Federal Government level.

We need to decentralize decisionmaking. The people spending the money need to be raising the money and spending it so that they can make the proper cost/benefit analysis. Highspeed rail is a good example of this.

You know, if California wants to raise its own money, as it has, with bonds, and go for highspeed rail, you know, good for them. Let them experiment. The rest of the country, the other 49 states can watch how well the system works and decide themselves whether they want to go down that road.

But the problem with federal intervention is it distorts the decisionmaking by state and local governments. And one good example of this, for example, is federal grants for urban transit. A lot of money over the years has gone to lightrail. Cities have gone for lightrail systems when bus systems would probably be more efficient, because the Federal Government pays the capital costs. The lightrail systems have high capital costs. Cities figure, well, let's grab the federal money for the capital costs for the lightrail, even though really in the long term bus systems are usually always more efficient.

So I am really concerned about the problem when the Federal Government intervenes. It distorts the more efficient state and local decisionmaking.

Senator Coats. How do we get around the—when I talk to mayors, governors, and others, they say, you know, so much of our early cost, and so much of the decisionmaking and the timelines are skewed simply because we continue to run into lengthy, almost never-ending environmental impact statement challenges to those, and so forth. We have that going on in our state right now, as well as the permitting process.

I would like to have whoever wants to speak to that.

Governor Rendell. Well, again, you did a good job of that in MAP–21, and the President's Executive Order cutting the timelines for environmental impact statements. Some of them take seven, eight years to complete.

Senator Coats. Right.

Governor Rendell. There is no reason under God's good earth that it cannot be done in six months. You know, if you tell people they have got unlimited time, they will use unlimited time. If you tell——

Senator Coats. Sounds a lot like Congress.

[Laughter.]

Governor Rendell. Well, right. I always use the example, if someone comes into a law firm and says I need an opinion letter and I need it next Tuesday, and the head of the firm says: Oh, well this is a respectable firm and we could never do it in that short period of time.

He pulls out of his pocket a cashier's check for a million dollars? They get it done. They get it done.

If you give six months for an EIS to be completed, with only the most stringent waiver provision, it is amazing how it would get done. When we prepared for stimulus, I wanted Pennsylvania to spend our money quickly because I knew the stimulative effect on roads and bridges.

I called my contractors in. I said, you usually get six months to respond to an RFP. You have two months. You've told me nobody is working, so you've got two months.

I said to my bureaucrats, you usually take six to nine months to award. You've got two months. And we had people working with stimulus dollars in three months. Congressman Oberstar's committee ranked the states on how quickly they spent the transportation stimulus money and we were tied for first with three other states.

It can be done. It can be done. That is where Congress can I think really do something terrific by insisting that it gets done.

Senator Coats. I want Mr. Poole to respond, but I just want to say, Governor, with your permission I want to take some of those quotes that you just said. I'll make sure you have attribution for those quotes, but I am going to be repeating quotes of a Democrat Governor all over the State of Indiana.

Governor Rendell. No question.

Mr. Poole. I think the Governor's points about getting the time for environmental reviews much shorter illustrates that we made some progress with MAP–21, but it isn't really where we need to go. It should be much shorter than that with time-certain time periods.

But it is also the question that I raised briefly of the higher cost of a federal dollar. Many states will not take federal money—you know, they try very hard not to use federal dollars on highway projects unless they absolutely need it because, "Buy America," Davis-Bacon, these other things that Congress has imposed mean the cost is much higher.

And now, with Buy America, FHWA has administratively decided that now it applies to utility relocations, as well, that everything that is used in a utility relocation has to be made in America. Utility companies have no idea where their stuff is made. They do not have the inventory system to do this. So it is threatening to hold up billions and billions of dollars of transportation projects over a new administrative interpretation.

Senator Coats. Thank you.

Mr. Delaney.

Representative Delaney. Thank you, Senator Coats.

I will use my time now, and then I will turn it over to my friend from New York.

You know, as we listen to the conversation that we have just had and we talk about the scale of the infrastructure challenges we have in this country, which also symmetrically indicates that we have a huge opportunity in this country to make this investment and get Americans to work, it is clear that this problem that we have is a multi-dimensional problem—meaning, we have it for a variety of reasons.

We have it for political reasons. We have it for financial reasons—in other words, there has not been sufficient money allocated against some of these issues. And we have it, quite frankly, because the world has moved very quickly. And the infrastructure is a long lead, long tail business and there have been rapid changes in the world particularly in the last 20 or 25 years that, particularly around logistics and communications and energy, et cetera, have accelerated much faster than people could reasonably have predicted. So there are lots of reasons we have these problems, which to me means we should have multiple solutions against this problem. The classic, you know, we need many tools in the toolkit.

And in my opinion, this issue should be our central, and I think, Governor, you said this very well in your testimony—should be our central economic domestic priority. And all of the solutions that we have heard: increasing privatization, reducing regulatory burden, coming up with a variety of infrastructure financing tools, should all be considered very seriously because they are probably all needed.

As the Governor said, the cost of doing nothing is in fact not nothing, and we are paying that price, and we should be putting our shoulder against all of these things. Because in fact they pencil out.

This is actually a really good investment for us to be making in this country. As Mr. Edwards said, we should not be making all this investment. A lot of it can be done by the private sector, and we should be laying that groundwork. But at the end of the day, there will be certain core governmental investments that have to be made. There are certain core financings that have to be made.

One of the things we have tried to work on with our legislation is also thinking about the time horizon.

Because to some extent I think this notion of shovel-ready projects, while it is catchy and it makes sense, does not always correlate with good infrastructure policy.

Because in fact if you travel around the country and you look at decisions that have been made around infrastructure, even if they will take years to actually implement because of the scale of the projects, create really good economic activity immediately because people know they are going to happen.

In other words, if there is a commitment to widen a port and it is going to take five or six years to do it, even with an accelerated approval process, et cetera, everything will start changing around that port, which is why we have tried to come up with an entity that can operate in a disconnected way from the normal political cycle.

So, maybe, Governor, I would be interested in your views on how we should think about the timeframe for some of these projects, and planning in general, and then maybe Mr. Edwards maybe you would comment on that, as well.

Governor Rendell. Well in terms of the timeframe, right now if you read the ASCE report we need to fix it first. Although we do need new capacity—I mean, there is a stunning statistic that since 1980 our percentage of vehicles on the road has increased by 104 percent. Since 1980, our lane capacity has increased by 4 percent.

So we need to expand our infrastructure. But first we need to fix it. And the good thing about fix-it-first is it is very stimulative because you do not have to go through EISes. The reason I was able to get work done in three months is because we were fixing bridges. We were fixing roads. There is very little—there is no requirement for an EIS at all. So you can get to those projects quickly.

Right now, the biggest challenge for America is to fix what we have. I mean, again I hope you can get your staff to read the full ASCE report. It is outright frightening, frightening and disturbing. So if you fix it first, that is going to speed up the timeline.

For projects, one thing I would differ with Mr. Edwards on is there has to be an entity to help fund regional projects. So it does no good for let's say the State of Pennsylvania to put in a rail system that goes through to Ohio, and then all the way up to Minnesota let's say, with one type of new technology. If Ohio is going to have a new type of technology, that will not work. The trains will not be able to run if we have a MagLev system and they have a conventional highspeed system.

So there has got to be a vehicle for those projects. So there has got to be long-term vision with good controls and good speed mechanisms, but fix it first is going to solve a lot of our problems.

Representative Delaney. Mr. Edwards, very quickly.

Mr. Edwards. You touched on something really important, which is it is not the short-term jobs, which is often the focus in Washington. It is long-term efficiency. With seaports, we need to make them more efficient.

The issue is not the short-term Army Corps of Engineer jobs dredging seaports, it is the long-term efficiency that our manufacturers and producers can have more efficient seaports to take the bigger ships that are coming with the bigger Panama Canal. That is the issue.

And with seaports, for example, they can be fully privatized. Britain has fully privatized most of its seaports. The top seaports in the world—Hong Kong and Singapore—are private. The advantage is, in a private company they see customer demand rising, they see the shipping demand rising, they go out to the market and they raise capital. They do the work. They do not have to go to Washington to lobby. If you have private ports, they can get things done quickly.

Representative Delaney. Right. Thank you.

Governor Rendell. But they can't dredge. And the most difficult thing that the Atlantic ports have to do is dredge to the depth that can accept those big ships coming through the Panama Canal. Only 2 of our 12 Eastern ports are dredged sufficiently to do that. We are going to lose a whole boatload of business to Canada because of that.

Representative Delaney. It is a really important point.

I want to turn it over now to my good friend from New York who actually happens to know a lot about transportation, Congressman Hanna.

Representative Hanna. And you are right, we ought to use the money that is in the Harbor Trust Fund. I mean, it is just sitting there as an offset, as opposed to what it is intended to do.

Explicit in this conversation is the notion that the private sector is so much more efficient than the public sector. We know the public sector does not pay taxes on its property. We know that it can issue low-cost bonds, and we are all agreed that, generally speaking, the Federal Government, with all its rules and prescriptive things that it impugns on local and state communities, really add to the overall cost.

Yet we also know that private businesses need an internal, or just a basic rate of return. I want to ask you. If we go forward with this, say take an airport, we are basically creating mini-monopolies that have long-term projected income streams and long-term projected debt streams, and all based on the assumption that the government cannot do it as well—which I believe.

I want to ask you, Mr. Edwards, what do you think the marginal capacity for those rates of return is based on your understanding, and anyone, about the general inefficiency of government? And Davis-Bacon aside, and other things like that, which I think are not something that, politically, we are not going to change in my opinion.

So what do you think?

Mr. Edwards. I am not sure exactly what your question is, but I mean private investors, there is absolutely no doubt that it is absolutely crucial. They want to earn profits. The search for profits induces efficiency. It makes companies try to reduce costs and maximize the customer's——

Representative Hanna. Well, Mr. Rendell, Governor Rendell has said that there are 1,500 private airports out of thousands of airports, correct? Somebody must have looked at those and said these are the viable ones for the private sector to take over. The rest are not.

I guess what I am asking is, does anybody have an idea of how inefficient government is vis-a-vis the private sector?

Mr. Edwards. There have been some comparison studies of the P3s, for example, on traditional government contracting. I mean, there is an Australian study, actually I think I've got right here, that compared a couple dozen P3s to traditional government contracting. And there is no doubt that private-sector companies, they get stuff done on time and on budget.

The Capital Beltway P3, for example, was finished last year on time and on budget because there was a strong incentive. If private actors put in their own equity, they've got to keep the costs low. They've got to make things finish on time.

Representative Hanna. So two possibilities exist here. We have a, take 20 percent if you want an internal rate of 10, so the public benefit arguably could be that difference, that 10 percent; it could be much wider. But we could enjoy both of those benefits. We could clean up our own mess.

Because we run the risk of being too prescriptive going forward even to private organizations, plus we run the risk of creating these mini-monopolies over some local bridge that maybe the math was wrong and these review boards that were done locally were not adequate.

Governor Rendell. Well the key on private/public partnerships, Congressman, and your point is well taken, but the key is the eventual contract. We tried to lease the Pennsylvania Turnpike, and my legislature, my Republican Legislature, turned it down because they wanted to control the patronage. They did not want to turn it over to a private entity.

We got a $12.8 billion bid from Citibank and Albertus. When the recession hit, they would have been holding the bag with the risk, but the taxpayers of Pennsylvania would have gotten a great deal. But the key there is the contract.

When you lease—you don't "sell" to a private entity, you lease it. And then you have in the lease the same rights than an owner who leases his house has. You have oversight. You put in maintenance standards they have to meet.

So it depends on the level of government oversight. But the real savings come on the operational side, because the private sector can and almost always—almost always; there are some exceptions—operates at a lower cost because of union costs, and not necessarily it's going to be nonunion, but because of existing contracts, because of the number of people who are in a workforce, they can reduce that; because they've got money to invest in technology faster than the government does.

So it is the operational nut. When they figure out what their rate of return has to be, they are talking about revenue but they are also figuring out how they—what percentage they can cut costs, and those two things factor in together.

Representative Hanna. Airports in France, Mr. Poole, how do they compare to ours? We know that there are a great many private.

Mr. Poole. Well, actually in France the airports are still largely government airports. Aeroports de Paris has sold about a third of the equity to investors, but the government still owns the majority share.

Airports in the UK are mostly privatized, but they do—the largest ones, where there are monopoly problems, they do have utility regulation on the prices they can charge. So it is similar to what we do with electric utilities in this country because, again, of monopoly issues, having some form of government oversight.

Representative Hanna. Have there been studies done on the differences between say how we do in our airports, what they cost, and those elsewhere?

Mr. Poole. There have been a few. There is a very good study out of the University of BC in Canada that looked at a database of almost 200 airports worldwide and concluded that the ones that were—that had either majority private, or 100 percent private ownership that could include a long-term lease, were more productive, more efficient in terms of operating, and that the least productive were full government ownership and multi-function port authorities, unfortunately, for the New York Port Authority.

Representative Hanna. Thank you. My time has expired.

Mr. Puentes. If I can just jump in, I think this conversation is very important. I think what I would like to take away from this is that we need to get away from just this idea of either things being public or private, and this rigid kind of notion of privatization.

What we see emerging throughout the country is an awful lot of innovation that is happening outside the Beltway—the states, metropolitan areas, cities, all working with the private sector in cases where it may or may not fit.

I mean, so all projects, as you mentioned are not going to be appropriate for private interest. They're not going to raise revenue. They're just not interested in those kinds of projects.

So what I would like to see happen is to kind of get to where it is this mix, where it is not the Federal Government on top kind of working with states and metropolitan areas, but it is all mixed up with the private sector. And some projects are going to make sense, and some are not.

So the BC example is a great model. There is something called Partnerships BC in British Columbia where when they are evaluating projects they have to decide whether or not a private entity is going to make sense for this.

So they have to look all across the board. Sometimes it is going to work, sometimes it is not. So I just want us to get past the notion that it is either going to be private or it is going to be public, and one is better than the other. It is very complex. There are lots of different projects out there, and it really depends on what we are trying to do.

Governor Rendell. And if you widen it beyond just transportation—take drinking water, a big problem—EPA estimates we are going to have to spend $335 billion in the next 20 years to put our drinking water in decent condition to preserve it.

There are some rich areas. You go into Lower Merion Pennsylvania and there is not a private water company in the world that would not want to provide the water to Lower Merion. But you tell them they are going to provide the water to parts of north Philadelphia and there would be no bidders. There would be no bidders because there is no revenue to support increased rates.

So again, there is no one size that fits all. But I think the point we are all making, Democrats and Republicans, the witnesses, we are all making that the private sector has to be an option going forward—one of the arrows we have in our quiver, there is no question about that.

Vice Chair Klobuchar [presiding]. Very good. I know Representative Delaney had some additional questions.

Representative Delaney. Yes, I thought that was a very good discussion. And I think we also should be thinking about public/private partnerships both on a project level, which I think is the historical kind of framing for how we think about these things, but also to some extent on a more macro level.

One of the things we have tried to do with our legislation is fund an infrastructure bank by effectively creating a giant public/private partnership. In other words, it is funded by private capital and provides a tax incentive by allowing companies to repatriate earnings. But again, done in a very market-based approach where we actually auction off the bonds, and we actually get the best deal for the taxpayer by doing it that way.

But the other—and, Mr. Poole, the other observation or question I had for you is: We all need to think about efficiencies in terms of how we finance these activities. One of the things we have tried to focus on in our legislation is having the infrastructure bank, for lack of a better term, be more of a bond guarantor.

Because it seems to me, while it may make sense in other countries to lend directly to the projects, in our country local governments have the ability to issue debt on a tax-exempt basis. And for as long as that exists, which I hope it exists for a very long time, that is a very advantageous way for local governments to borrow money. And to the extent we have a larger financial support enterprise, it should be actually guaranteeing their debt, as opposed to lending directly because of the efficiencies.

I don't know if you have any views on that?

Mr. Poole. Yes, I agree, Congressman. I think that is a very important point. We used to have bond insurance for infrastructure kinds of projects in this country until the financial crisis. And Ambac and others basically went out of business at that point.

So there is a gap in the market right now that really would be much better for infrastructure investment if there were the kind of bond insurance, or analogous bond insurance that used to exist before the financial crisis.

So that is another point that I like about your proposal, is that that is a gap that needs to be filled and it would help a lot.

Representative Delaney. And, Mr. Edwards, you talked about how local governments should be driving a lot of these decisions, which I agree with. I don't think they should be driving all the decisions because some of these decisions are inherently federal and multi-jurisdictional and of national importance, but the model where local governments really have a say in determining their own infrastructure. And when you think about infrastructure banks proposals, or in our situation more of a bond guarantor, which is more geared towards local governments, do you see this being more of an enterprise that operates against a national strategy? Or do you think these enterprises would be better if they are focused on serving the needs of local municipalities?

Mr. Edwards. I haven't looked at your legislation in detail, but I mean for me the decisionmaking should be where the money is raised and money is spent. If different people are raising the money than spending it, you get bad decisionmaking. So I just like to see decentralized decisionmaking, which to me means decentralized financing and ownership.

Representative Delaney. Right. Well those are all my questions. I just want to again add my thanks to Governor Rendell, Mr. Poole, Mr. Puentes, and Mr. Edwards for their thoughtful testimony and for carving out their time. It was a terrific discussion.

Vice Chair Klobuchar. Thank you. And just one last question I have is just how maintenance fits in with this.

I always think about when we do these ribbon-cuttings for a new transit project, or a new bridge, and when you fix a pothole there's not usually a bunch of people celebrating. And so—or you fix a gusset under a bridge.

How do you think the road maintenance and the bridge maintenance fits into all of this, Mr. Poole, and then Mr. Rendell.

Mr. Poole. Two answers to that. One is that a growing number of state DOTs are having great success with competitively contracting for highway maintenance. Virginia is one of the pioneers plus Texas and Florida. And so that is a way in which you can often get more value, more maintenance per dollar spent than doing it with state employees.

But the other is a point I made briefly, and you may have been out of the room when this came up, is that if you do long-term infrastructure PPPs where the entity created to finance, build, and operate the project also maintains it over a life that may be anywhere from 30 years to 75 or 99 years, so you basically create a guaranteed source of maintenance funding in those kinds of long-term arrangements.

So if you think of the overall highway responsibilities of a state DOT, if 20 percent of that can be converted to long-term P3s, that whole sector then is guaranteed for a long period of time to be properly maintained. And the state in an annual budget sense only has to come up with, you know, be responsible for looking at the maintenance for the rest of it. So I think that is an advantage of the long-term P3s that is often not fully appreciated.

Vice Chair Klobuchar. Governor?

Governor Rendell. First I want to correct one thing Mr. Poole said. Most states, I would say 95 percent, almost 100 percent of the maintenance as well as the building work is done by private contractors. The state workers are usually doing oversight or a little bit of painting, but we bid out everything. Pennsylvania bids out everything, maintenance as well as new construction.

Let me just give you an example of one area in response to your question. I–95 runs through the City of Philadelphia for 18 miles. There are 14 bridges in those 18 miles that I–95 goes over. It is estimated to put those bridges, most of which are either structurally deficient or functionally obsolete, into fair, decent, safe condition would cost $4.5 billion.

The City of Philadelphia's entire capital budget for everything—police stations, fire stations, rec centers, road paving—is $120 million a year.

Now there are two ways to do that. If we were allowed to toll I–95—we can't because it is a previously accredited federal highway—they grandfathered the states that already tolled it, but we can't—we would have a chance to raise some of that money.

Or, alternatively, we are going to need federal investment. And that is just maintaining. But it is maintaining the Nation's largest highway. It is a state and local responsibility and we need help.

Vice Chair Klobuchar. Okay. Very good.

I see Representative Maloney is here. If you want to ask a few questions, then we are going to end, I think.

Representative Maloney. Everything is happening at once. We had votes in Financial Services, and then we had votes in Government Reform and Oversight.

I just feel that infrastructure is so important, why are we not investing more in infrastructure? It creates good jobs. In the district that I am privileged to represent, I have two major construction projects—the 2nd Avenue Subway and the Eastside Connector—both of which have over $4 billion in federal funds and are creating over 40,000 jobs.

My question really is on highspeed rail. Our country used to lead the world in infrastructure, and now we are falling apart. When you go to Europe, to China, to India, they all have highspeed rail.

And particularly on the Northeast Corridor, it would be a corridor that makes money now for Amtrak, and it would make money if we had highspeed rail between—I see Governor Rendell—between Philadelphia and Washington and New York, to Boston, all of this area.

Your thoughts on how to move this forward. Do you think it would be possible to do a public/private match that would be able to protect the union agreements, but would also give us the money to move forward? It is obviously a financing deal. And there has been a debate in Congress over an infrastructure bank.

Some people support it as a financing mechanism. Others say it is just another level of bureaucracy. If you want to fund it, float your bonds. Float your financing system and just move forward. What do you need an infrastructure bank for?

I would like to open it up for answers and questions. We did get a highspeed rail downpayment of $300 million between New York and Boston, which I find very exciting. But comments on those?

Governor Rendell. Congresswoman, I think I can speak for all four of us. We all endorsed the concept of the infrastructure bank. We may have some differences about how it should operate, et cetera, but we all endorsed the concept.

In terms of what you're saying, a Northeast Corridor highspeed rail could not be a better example of a PPP. Let me preface this by saying I am on the advisory board of Japanese MagLev, which if it were instituted on the East Coast you could get from New York to Washington in 59 minutes, Philadelphia to New York in 23 minutes. They are opening up in Japan in November a 310-mile-an-hour MagLev system, and they want to construct it, and they are willing to put up part of the funding.

It should be like the TIGER grant. The Federal Government should put up part of the funding. The majority of the funding should come from the private sector. But the states that benefit from it should also put up part of the funding.

We wanted to expand the Philadelphia to Harrisburg Rail Line. Amtrak, while I was Governor, wanted to put $75 million in. I matched the $75 million. We cut the travel time from 120 minutes, 2 hours, to 90 minutes. We increased ridership from 900,000 to 1.2 million.

If we had highspeed rail in the Northeast Corridor, you could end the shuttles, the air shuttles. It would do so much for tarmac waiting time to get rid of those shuttles. We ought to be doing this. It ought to be our first big infrastructure bank PPP partnership.

You would have not only the Japanese MagLev people, but you would have a lot of bidders from the private sector. I think we all agree with that. The private sector would be happy to come in and bid for that.

Mr. Edwards. I would just note, if I may, that most highspeed rail lines in the world do not make money. And the Northeast Corridor, you know absolutely passenger rail probably would make sense.

The problem, if the Federal Government gets heavily involved in funding highspeed rail on the Northeast Corridor, every state in the Union is going to want federal money for their own highspeed rail lines through areas that make—where it makes a lot less sense.

So this is a problem with federal involvement, that there is always the political problem that people want the money shared around, and yet customer demand wise, highspeed rail may only make sense in some areas like the Boston to Washington.

Governor Rendell. Well the Acela makes money, and Lord knows how much money a highspeed rail line would make. But that is the job of the infrastructure bank. You insulate the infrastructure bank from political pressure, like the BRAC Commission, which by and large works pretty well. Philadelphia has been the unfortunate negative recipient of a lot of BRAC, so I know it works pretty well.

[Laughter.]

You insulate it, and you have those decisions made on a cost/benefit analysis. He is absolutely right. The Northeast Corridor is the first project we should try. If that makes money, then maybe we examine California to Oregon and see if that would make money. And then we examine the Midwest and see if that would make money.

But everyone knows that if the Acela makes money, and it does as a standalone, you know highspeed rail would make money.

Vice Chair Klobuchar. All right, one last answer.

Mr. Puentes.

Mr. Puentes. We need to think differently about the partnerships. I mean, the Japanese examples are great because it is not just the rail line in which the company is investing, it is real estate deals around the Tokyo train station, 3 million passengers a day, whatever it is. That is all a real estate deal also owned by the railway company.

So we've got to get beyond just thinking about these as individual structure projects and think about it more as economy shaping type projects.

Vice Chair Klobuchar. Well thank you. That is a great way to end. I want to thank our witnesses, excellent job. We had great attendance, once again, at this hearing. And I know that there is a lot of work that needs to be done.

We have people right up here, including Representative Delaney, and Senator Warner, and others who are devoted to getting something done on the infrastructure bank part of this.

But as we have discussed with Governor Rendell, there are also other things we need to do with bonding and other things that I think could be very positive.

So we are excited to move ahead with this, and I hope it will be one of our top bipartisan efforts in the coming year.

It should be, and it will be. Thank you very much, and the record will stay open for the next two weeks, and the hearing is adjourned.

(Whereupon, at 11:03 a.m., Wednesday, July 24, 2013, the hearing was adjourned.)

SUBMISSIONS FOR THE RECORD

PREPARED STATEMENT OF HON. AMY KLOBUCHAR, VICE CHAIR, JOINT ECONOMIC COMMITTEE

I want to thank everyone for being here this morning to discuss the critical need to strengthen and improve our nation's infrastructure system.

I'd like to introduce our distinguished panel of witnesses, who have a wealth of experience and insight in this area:

Edward Rendell was Governor of Pennsylvania from 2003 to 2011 and previously served two terms as the Mayor of Philadelphia. He is a co-founder and co-chair of Building America's Future, which focuses on the need for more significant investment in infrastructure to ensure America maintains its place as a global economic leader.

Robert Poole is the Searle Freedom Trust Transportation Fellow and director of transportation policy at the Reason Foundation. Mr. Poole, an MIT-trained engineer, has advised both Democratic and Republican administrations.

Robert Puentes is a senior fellow with the Brookings Institution Metropolitan Policy Program, where he also directs the program's Metropolitan Infrastructure Initiative. He is an expert on transportation and infrastructure, urban planning, growth management, suburban issues and housing.

Chris Edwards is the director of tax policy studies at the Cato Institute. He is an expert on federal and state tax and budget issues. Mr. Edwards previously served as a senior economist with the Joint Economic Committee.

If you look back through American history, many of the greatest periods of growth and progress were made possible by historic investments in infrastructure.

We connected the East and the West Coasts by rail in 1869, ushering in the Second Industrial Revolution.

We began building the interstate highway system in the 1950s, connecting our country and our economy in ways never before possible ... and we did it, by the way, with a Democratic Congress and Republican President Dwight D. Eisenhower in the White House.

America is the country it is today because we've been willing to invest in the foundations for growth, innovation and commerce. In recent years, however, we've fallen behind. The World Economic Forum ranked American infrastructure 6th in the world in its 2007–2008 report. Five years later, we have slipped to 25th place.

The cracks in our broken transportation system became tragically clear in my home state on the afternoon of August 1, 2007, when on the I–35W bridge collapsed into the Mississippi River ... taking the lives of thirteen and injuring many more.

As I said that day, a bridge should not just fall down in the middle of America ... .especially not an eight-lane interstate highway, which is one of the most heavily traveled bridges in the state ... especially not at rush hour in the heart of a major metropolitan area ... especially not a bridge six blocks from my house that I drive over with my family every day.

I was with Secretary of Transportation Anthony Foxx in Minnesota last Monday, and pointed out that the I–35W bridge was rebuilt on-budget and in just 9 months ... well ahead of schedule. How were we able to do it so quickly? Because we had a bipartisan group of leaders working around the clock at the state, local and federal level.

But our infrastructure problems are by no means limited to just bridges.

According to the American Society of Civil Engineers 2013 Report Card, the U.S scores a D or worse in aviation, dams, drinking water, levees, roads, schools and transit. Our bridges and rail system score a C+, while our ports get a C. We cannot be satisfied with "failing," or even "average," and we need to improve our grades now.

We know this is a matter of public safety, but it is also a matter of economic competitiveness.

The reason American businesses can operate anywhere, including in rural areas, is because our past investments in transportation infrastructure allow them to get their products to markets around the world.

Compared to other countries, we're now underinvesting in these networks: China and India are spending about 9% and 8%, respectively, of their GDPs. Europe spends 5%, while we are spending only about 2%.

This strategy is penny-wise and pound-foolish, saving dollars in the short term while undermining our global competitiveness in the long term.

And in fact, faulty transportation infrastructure is expected to drive up the cost of doing business in America by an estimated $430 billion in the next decade.

What we need now are smart, targeted solutions to ensure our nation's infrastructure is safe, strong and efficient.

I introduced a bill last Congress called the Rebuild America Jobs Act, which would have gotten the ball rolling on desperately needed infrastructure investments, in part by creating a national infrastructure bank—an idea that has historically won bipartisan support as well as the backing of everyone from the AFL–CIO to the Chamber of Commerce.

While we weren't able to bring that particular proposal across the finish line, we have made good progress in other areas:

Over the last four years, we've improved over 350,000 miles of roads and more than 6,000 miles of rail.

We've repaired or replaced over 20,000 bridges.

We passed a bipartisan highway bill last year that has paved the way for critical infrastructure improvements across the county.

And back in May, the Senate passed the Water Resources Development Act (WRDA), which would strengthen our nation's water infrastructure and make crucial upgrades to our ports, harbors, locks and dams. WRDA includes many provisions of the RIVER Act, which I introduced with Senator Casey to improve our nation's inland waterways.

So we are moving in the right direction. But we're here today because we still have more to do.

There are several good ideas out there, including a number of bond proposals and efforts to establish an infrastructure bank. Senator Warner and Representative Delaney, both members of this Committee, have been leaders in putting new ideas forward and I know we'll be hearing about some of those ideas today.

Ultimately, this is about strengthening our economy. America must be a country that makes stuff again, that invents things, that exports to the world. Whether it's roads, bridges, transit, airports or waterways, the need to rebuild our infrastructure is critical to reclaiming our country's competitive edge ... to getting workers back on the job ... and to ensuring the safety of our people.

I'd like to thank our witnesses for being here, and I look forward to hearing their testimony. Now I would like to yield 2 minutes to Representative Delaney.

PREPARED STATEMENT OF SENATOR DANIEL COATS

Thank you Senator Klobuchar, and I am pleased to be here today for what is a very important hearing because, to use an infrastructure term, we are at a cross-roads.

As a nation, our infrastructure is in a deplorable state according to many recent reports. Our funding mechanisms have broken down, and we are failing to maintain what we have, let alone build the 21st Century infrastructure that we need. The fact is that our current fiscal crisis prevents us from having the ability to invest more federal dollars on these vital projects, largely because of spiraling mandatory spending. Meanwhile, several of our global competitors have turned to innovative private financing options to cover their shortfalls. Australia, Canada, the EU, and the United Kingdom already rely heavily on private investment, with hundreds of privately financed infrastructure projects already up and running or in the works. The U.S. is far behind the curve on private investment in infrastructure, and unless this is addressed it will only continue to impede our economic growth and competitiveness.

The need to address our infrastructure crisis is urgent. The Panama Canal widening will be completed in the next two years, and with it will come container ships calling on America's ports that are almost double the size of today's vessels. We expect to see freight movement in this country double over the next 20 years. This explosion in freight movement comes with additional jobs that grow communities. But as we face this dynamic growth over the next 20 years, we as a nation do not have a comprehensive strategy to address these expanded infrastructure needs at our seaports, on our railways, and across our highways, bridges and roads. Our user fee systems are broken. Our permitting processes are costly, both in time and money. The cost of our inaction is jobs and growth, as global competitors like China, India, and Brazil make expensive and necessary investments across their entire infrastructure.

I'm going to brag about my Hoosier State for a minute, where freight movement is such a critical part of our economy. Seventy-five percent of the United States and Canadian populations, over 261 million people, live within one day's truck drive of Indiana. Each year, 724 million tons of freight travel through Indiana, making it the 5th busiest state for commercial freight traffic.

We have a network of more than 680 commercial and general aviation airports, including the 6th largest cargo airport in the nation at Indianapolis International Airport.

Indiana ranks 15th in the nation in total foreign and domestic waterborne shipping with 67.5 million tons, 4th in total freight railroads, and 9th among all states for railroad mileage.

Indiana is 1st in the nation for interstate highway access with 14 interstates, 1st in the nation in pass-through interstates, and 10th in the nation in rail tons originated with over 50 million tons. In short, Indiana is America's crossroads.

As such, we recognized early on how important infrastructure is to our economy, and how we had to continually maintain and expand our infrastructure. Indiana was one of the early adapters in our country in the use of innovative financing mechanisms for transportation and infrastructure.

Indiana established itself early on as a national leader in leveraging private sector capital and innovation to improve existing infrastructure and build new infrastructure. The Indiana General Assembly passed legislation over the last several years authorizing the Indiana Finance Authority to enter into public-private partnerships, or "P3s." Our first P3 was the 2006 lease of the Indiana Toll Road. The second P3 project is the East End Crossing, which will link Indiana 265 in Utica, Indiana, with Kentucky 841 in Prospect, Kentucky. The East End Crossing will complete the I–265 outer beltway around the Louisville metro area and create economic development opportunities in southern Indiana.

We're also working on another high profile P3, the Illiana Corridor. Illiana is a bi-state expressway project in northwest Indiana and northeastern Illinois. Given its central location in the nation, the northwest Indiana and northeastern Illinois region is heavily utilized by three sectors of travel: roadways, rail, and air. This region is also experiencing substantial growth in population and employment. Population in the Illiana study area is projected to grow by 175%, and with it employment will increase 225%. As a national link to transportation and commerce, we see heavy use of our highways. As a commerce hub, our region is benefitting from the expansion of large inland ports for logistics and intermodal transfer and logistics. I fully support this effort and I commend Governor Mike Pence and Governor Pat Quinn for their leadership on this critical infrastructure project.

In 2005 our then-Governor, Mitch Daniels, launched an aggressive 10-year transportation plan called Major Moves. Major Moves significantly improved and expanded Indiana's highway infrastructure. A total of $2.6 billion was committed to Major Moves from the long-term lease of the Indiana Toll Road and the plan called for 104 new roadways by 2015 with 1,600 lane miles. No additional debt or increase in taxes has been incurred to complete Major Moves projects.

By the end of calendar year 2012, we invested over $7.5 billion in construction and, among other things, accomplished the following:

- 65 roadway projects were complete or substantially under construction;
- 19 roadway projects were accelerated—when compared to the original 2006 plan;
- We completed 375 new centerline miles, 48 new or reconstructed interchanges, and 5,030 preservation centerline miles accounting for 40 percent of the state's inventory;
- We rehabilitated or replaced 720 bridges, 13 percent of the state's inventory, and anticipate by 2015 having completed rehabilitation or replacement of 1,070 bridges comprising 20 percent of the state's inventory.

Between 2001 and 2005, prior to Major Moves, the state averaged nearly $750 million for construction per year. Of that $750 million, an average of nearly $250 million per year was spent on new construction while an average of approximately $500 million per year was spent on preservation projects. Backed by Major Moves funding, INDOT averaged more than $1 billion in construction dollars invested annually between 2005 and 2012.

Why did Indiana take these steps? Because Hoosiers were tired of waiting for Congress to act. America is tired of waiting for Congress to Act. And the longer Congress waits to act, the more jobs will go to China, Mexico, India, Brazil, and our global competitors.

I recognize that, predominantly, the solution to this funding problem in the Senate lies within the jurisdiction of the Finance and Environment and Public Works Committees, but the fact of the matter is we need to find a solution and we need to find it quickly.

We have a fundamental problem with regards to the depletion of the highway trust fund as a result of a broken motor fuel user fee system. We need smart, innovative out of the box solutions.

The Hoosier model works, and I believe it is a "best practices" example of what can happen when the legislative and executive branch can come together in a bipartisan way with out of the box, innovative proposals. I would encourage the members of the Senate to look to Indiana as a blueprint for success in this area, and I look forward to hearing from the witnesses.

———

PREPARED STATEMENT OF HON. EDWARD G. RENDELL, FORMER GOVERNOR, PENNSYLVANIA

Vice Chair Klobuchar and Members of the Committee, thank you for the opportunity to testify before you on the urgent need for federal infrastructure investment. This hearing could not be more important as I believe this issue is one of the most urgent facing our country.

I am here today as a co-chair of Building America's Future, an organization that I co-founded with Mayor Michael Bloomberg and former Governor Arnold Schwarzenegger. Together, we represent a diverse and bipartisan coalition of state and local officials working to advance infrastructure investment to promote economic growth, global competitiveness and better quality of life for all Americans.

Eighty years ago Congress passed and President Franklin Roosevelt signed the National Industrial Recovery Act that was responsible for creating the Public Works Administration (PWA). Between 1933 and 1939 the PWA funded and administered the construction of 34,508 large-scale construction projects such as roads, dams, sewage treatment plants, ports, airports, schools, hospitals and even major warships for the Navy. Americans still rely on many of these projects to this very day including the Triborough Bridge, the Lincoln Tunnel, the Grand Coulee Dam and the Overseas Highway connecting Key West to the Florida mainland. With an investment of $6 billion, the PWA funded needed projects and employed thousands of skilled workers.

This era epitomized the American can-do spirit of building big things. We need to recapture that spirit because if we don't, we will continue to fall behind our economic competitors.

Late last year Building America's Future released Falling Apart and Falling Behind—a comparative analysis of the transportation infrastructure investments being made by the U.S. and our global economic competitors. As the title suggests, other countries are racing ahead of us by making smart, long-term investments in modern transportation networks such as rail, ports and electric grids to meet the demands of the 21st century global economy.

The fact that the World Economic Forum had ranked the competitiveness of U.S. infrastructure number one in 2005 and number fourteen in 2012 illustrates the challenges before us.

Take a look at some of the port investments being made by our global competitors in anticipation of post-Panamax vessels becoming the norm once the newly widened Panama Canal is completed. Since 2000, China has invested over $3.5 trillion in its ports. Brazil has invested over $250 billion since 2008. And as a result China is now home to six of the world's ten busiest container ports while the U.S. has none in the top ten. Shanghai's port now moves more container traffic in a year than the top eight U.S. ports combined. Brazil's investment has gone into its Acu Superport, larger than the island of Manhattan, with state-of-the-art highway, pipeline and conveyor-belt capacity to ease the transfer of raw materials onto ships heading to China.

Here at home, and despite a large surplus in the Harbor Maintenance Trust Fund, the busiest U.S. harbors are under-maintained. The U.S. Army Corps of Engineers estimates that full channel dimensions at the nation's busiest 59 ports are available less than 35 percent of the time. Only two of our ports on the East Coast are deep enough to accommodate the post-Panamax ships.

The situation on our roads is not much better. The Texas Transportation Institute's 2012 Urban Mobility Report stated that traffic congestion had Americans wasting time and 2.9 billion gallons of fuel at a cost of $121 billion—that equates to $818 per commuter. And no wonder when one learns that the number of vehicles traveling on American highways has increased by 37 percent from 1990 to 2010 yet the miles of new highway lanes have grown by only four percent. This comes at a time when the nation's population has increased by 25 percent.

The growing congestion on our railway system plagues the nation's freight corridors, choking economic growth and development throughout every region of the country. In Chicago alone, the nation's largest rail center, congestion is so bad that it takes a freight train longer to get through the city limits than it does to reach Los Angeles. The cost to mine metallurgical coal in North America is the same as it is in Australia, but the cost to ship it to the coasts so that it may be exported to Asia is up to four times greater due to transportation and logistical costs.

Earlier this year the American Society of Civil Engineers (ASCE) released its 2013 Report Card for America's Infrastructure and awarded America's infrastructure a grade of D+. In order to bring the nation's infrastructure up to a state of good repair, the ASCE estimates that it will take $3.6 trillion between now and 2020; $3.6 trillion—that is a very big number. But for America to remain competitive we must have a first class infrastructure. And that means all levels of government and the private sector must make strategic investments in infrastructure.

Many at the state and local levels are weary of waiting for Washington to act and have begun to take matters into their own hands. This year alone, four governors have signed legislation to increase revenue for transportation and several others had proposed similar measures. And the success rate for local ballot initiatives remains high. In 2012, the success rate of such initiatives was 79 percent.

The West Coast in particular has been a hotbed of innovation and activity. Earlier this month, the Oregon legislature approved a bill to allow drivers to pay a fee for each mile they drive instead of paying the state gasoline tax. The current state gas tax is 30 cents per gallon and would be replaced by a fee of 1.5 cents for every mile driven. The program is limited to 5,000 volunteer drivers who will have several options to report their mileage such as smartphone tracking, reading mileage from their car's odometer, and even paying a flat fee to address privacy concerns.

Late last year the states of Oregon, California, and Washington joined with British Columbia to form the West Coast Infrastructure Exchange. The intent of the Exchange is to combine expertise and resources to build projects critical to the region's economic growth and competitiveness. By combining several smaller projects that on their own may not attract private sector investment, the Exchange seeks to maximize investments of public and private sector dollars.

With regard to leveraging public investments with private dollars, more states have approved legislation granting them authority to pursue partnerships with the private sector. Currently 36 states and Puerto Rico have such authority.

In Chicago, Mayor Rahm Emanuel fought for and got approval to create the Chicago Infrastructure Exchange to leverage private capital with public funds to fix rundown schools and upgrade water systems.

But we still need leadership in Washington to help prioritize and fund large-scale projects of regional and national significance that are too large for any one state or community to handle. Without an overriding national vision and interconnected network, America's transportation infrastructure would resemble a patchwork of disconnected roads and rails; our aviation system would be untenable; and goods movement would be greatly hindered.

The impending expiration of MAP–21 in September of next year gives Congress an opportunity to continue to reform the nation's transportation policy and to get creative in raising the revenue necessary to keep America moving.

There is no way around it—more revenue is needed to keep the Highway Trust Fund solvent. The Congressional Budget Office has reported that "the current trajectory of the Highway Trust Fund is unsustainable." By 2015, the Highway Trust Fund will not have sufficient revenues to meet its obligations in both the highway and transit accounts. Without an increase in revenues or a reduction in expenditures or further transfers from the general fund, the cumulative shortfalls in the Highway Trust Fund will total $92 billion for the highway account and $43 billion for the transit account by the end of 2023.

To regain our economic status as a world leader and to ensure the quality of life that Americans have come to expect, Building America's Future recommends:

- Immediately creating a commission charged with producing a ten-year critical infrastructure plan—covering transportation, water, energy and broadband—that makes significant new investments. The Congressional Budget Office has concluded that an annual additional investment of $185 billion would be economically justified and the American Society of Civil Engineers recommends an investment of $200 billion over the next eight years to rebuild the American infrastructure;
- Passing a long-term transportation bill;
- Establishing a National Infrastructure Bank to, among other things, target federal dollars to economically strategic freight gateways and corridors and invest more strategically in projects of national or regional significance that will deliver real economic returns;
- Further increasing the authorization level of TIFIA;
- Making the TIGER program permanent;
- Raising or lifting the cap on Private Activity Bonds;

- Developing other ways to pay for building and maintaining our roads such as:
    —Incorporating congestion pricing and truck tolling arrangements to more adequately cover the costs imposed by highway use;
    —Lifting the federal ban on tolling interstates;
    —Reinstating Build America Bonds;
    —Fees based on miles traveled;
    —Reserves built into capital budgets;
    —Once the economy recovers, consider raising the federal gas tax and indexing it to inflation

The other option is to let the status quo prevail. We can continue to underinvest in our critical infrastructure. We can continue to sit on the sidelines and watch countries like Germany, Brazil and Canada make the investments in 21st century transportation networks and infrastructure. We can continue to "fall apart and fall behind."

Let me be clear. There is a cost associated with doing nothing. The American Society of Civil Engineers has recently issued a series of "Failure to Act" reports that compared current and projected needs for infrastructure investment against the current funding trends in surface transportation; water and wastewater; electricity; and airports, inland waterways and seaports. The final report, released this January, documents that the total cumulative gap between projected needs and likely investment in these important sectors will be $1.1 trillion by 2020. It further documents that aging and unreliable infrastructure will increase the costs to businesses by $1.2 trillion and to households by $611 billion by 2020.

Infrastructure is an economic driver and has the added benefit of creating long-term quality jobs. It improves the quality of our lives and it enhances our economic competitiveness. There is no better time to invest in America's future. We have seen interest rates at record lows thereby making it more attractive to build. But as the economy continues to recover, those rates will begin to rise and so will the costs to build and repair our nation's infrastructure. We must act now.

Thank you, Vice Chair Klobuchar for the opportunity to testify on this very important issue. I look forward to answering the committee's questions.

PREPARED STATEMENT OF ROBERT W. POOLE, JR., DIRECTOR OF TRANSPORTATION POLICY, REASON FOUNDATION

My name is Robert Poole, Director of Transportation Policy at the Reason Foundation. For more than three decades I have been researching privatization and public-private partnerships at local, state, and federal levels of government. My book, Cutting Back City Hall (1980), was the first book-length treatment of this subject at the city and county government level. For the last 15 years or so, my full-time focus has been on transportation infrastructure policy, both aviation and surface transportation. I am a member of two standing committees of the Transportation Research Board and am a member of the Government Accountability Office's National Aviation Studies Advisory panel. I am a member of the Air Traffic Control Association and serve on the board of the Public Private Partnership division of the American Road & Transportation Builders Association. I have advised the FAA, the FHWA, the FTA, and the Office of the Secretary of Transportation, as well as the White House Office of Policy Development and National Economic Council. I have also advised or consulted for half a dozen state DOTs.

THE UNITED STATES LAGS IN USING PUBLIC-PRIVATE PARTNERSHIPS IN INFRASTRUCTURE

We Americans pride ourselves as having an economy that is largely market-based with investor ownership of the means of production. Yet when it comes to infrastructure, and transportation infrastructure in particular, the United States is an outlier compared with our OECD allies. A major trend in recent decades—first in Europe, then Australia and New Zealand, and more recently Latin America—has been to privatize state-owned enterprises that provide major transportation infrastructure. By contrast, most U.S. transportation infrastructure continues to be state-owned enterprises of various kinds, with many of the limitations and disadvantages that we see in state-owned enterprises in China, developing countries, and parts of Europe that have not yet reformed such infrastructure.

In most developed countries, the primary model is the long-term franchise (usually termed a "concession" overseas), similar to U.S. practice for investor-owned electric utilities. A smaller number of airports, toll road systems, and seaports have been sold outright to investors. In either case, the transformation from government ownership and operation to investor ownership or concession operation brings a transition to direct charges (pricing) of the infrastructure, creating bondable revenue streams that facilitate long-term financing of long-lived capital investments. Revenue bond financing also ensures that the capital markets scrutinize the soundness of the investment, which tends to weed out poorly justified projects.

This model may sound familiar, because it is how U.S. toll roads and our larger airports are financed, despite being owned by government entities. But it is far removed from the way other U.S. transportation infrastructure is financed and managed. What follows is a brief overview contrasting the provision of five types of transportation infrastructure in the United States versus other developed countries.

Airports

Airports Council International recently reported that 450 commercial airports worldwide have some degree of private-sector participation in their management or ownership. In Europe alone, ACI–Europe reports that 48% of all passengers are handled at airports with either full or partial investor ownership as of 2010. There are 25 airport companies listed on stock exchanges, including two in Southeast Asia, three in Mexico, five in China, and the rest in Europe and Australasia. The United States has just one commercial airport that has been long-term leased under the FAA Airport Privatization Pilot Program (San Juan International), with a second one pending (Chicago Midway).

Air Traffic Control

Over 50 countries have corporatized their ATC providers since 1987. This means separating the ATC provider from the government's aviation safety regulator and from the government's budget, making it self-supporting from fees paid to it by airspace users. Most of these air navigation service providers (ANSPs) are government corporations, but as self-supporting entities, they can issue revenue bonds to finance capital modernization programs, unlike the unreformed FAA in this country. The larger ANSPs all have investment-grade bond ratings. Two of the ANSPs can be considered partially privatized: NATS in the UK, which is 49% owned by the government with the balance owned by aviation stakeholders (including employees) and Nav Canada, which is a not-for-profit company with a stakeholder governing board.

Highways and Bridges

In the 1960s when European countries began building national motorway systems, three of them—France, Italy, and Spain—chose to finance these new highways via toll revenues, and used a mix of state-owned and investor-owned companies to finance, build, own, and operate the new toll roads. Portugal later adopted a similar system. In the late 1990s and early 2000s, all four countries privatized their state-owned toll road companies, shifting them to long-term concession agreements. This long-term concession model was adopted by Australia in the 1980s to build tolled urban expressways in Sydney, Melbourne, and Brisbane. The model had spread to Latin America by the 1990s, with long-term toll concessions awarded in Argentina, Brazil, Chile, Colombia, Mexico, and Peru. It has also been used in China, Malaysia, the Philippines, and elsewhere in Asia. The United States is a late adopter of the concession model, with a handful of projects opened in the 1990s and a small but growing number in the 2000s, mostly in California, Florida, Texas, and Virginia.

Seaports

A global wave of port privatization begin with the sale in 1983 of 19 UK ports of the British Transport Docks Board as Associated British Ports. Other UK ports were sold in subsequent years. By 1997 a World Bank report found that a large majority of the 50 largest ports worldwide had either mixed or private (investor) ownership, with mixed ownership generally referring to the landlord port model in which the government owns the land and retains regulatory control while various private operators own and operate individual terminals. The United States has mostly landlord ports, with only a few totally state-owned and operated. Major U.S. seaports are largely self-supporting, but pay a Harbor Maintenance tax whose proceeds are used for Army Corps of Engineers harbor dredging projects.

Waterways

Most commercial waterways worldwide are government-owned and operated, but some of the largest are operated on a corporatized basis, including the Panama Canal and the Suez Canal. Both charge tolls for passage, and in the case of the current Panama Canal widening and modernization, this $5 billion project is being financed via revenue bonds based on the toll revenue. France is exploring the development of new inland canals and the refurbishment of existing ones as long-term PPPs. In the United States, the entire inland waterways system is managed by the

Army Corps of Engineers. Less than 10% of the cost of operating, maintaining, and improving the inland waterways system is paid for by commercial users, via a tax on diesel fuel; the rest is paid for by general federal revenues (i.e., all taxpayers). Waterways thus represent the most highly subsidized of all modes of goods-movement infrastructure in the United States.

Global Companies

Another difference between the United States and other OECD countries is a dearth of U.S. companies experienced not just in building but in owning, operating, and maintaining major transportation infrastructure such as airports, toll roads, and seaports. Of the world's 100 largest airport operators (as compiled by *Airline Business*), 36 are either fully or partially investor-owned—but not a single one is based in the United States. And in *Public Works Financing*'s annual listing of the world's 35 largest surface transportation infrastructure providers, only one (Fluor) is a U.S. company. Of the top five, three are from Spain, one from Australia, and one from France. Investor-owned transportation infrastructure is a large and growing global industry, but thus far US companies are at best bit players.

Investment Capital

According to the 2012 tabulation by *Infrastructure Investor*, over the last five years the 30 largest global infrastructure equity funds have raised nearly $172 billion to invest in privatized and PPP infrastructure. Over the decade ending in 2012, all such funds have raised an estimated $291 billion. When leveraged with debt in a typical project financing structure, this amount of equity could support nearly $1.2 trillion worth of infrastructure projects. That investment will go where it is welcome, and thus far the United States is seen as a difficult, emerging market. At least in this segment of infrastructure, US funds are playing a significant role, representing 37% of the infrastructure investment firms and about 30% of the capital raised. But since there are few opportunities so far to invest such funds productively here in the USA, much of their investment is overseas.

WHY DOES IT MATTER THAT THE UNITED STATES LAGS SO FAR BEHIND?

High quality infrastructure is essential for a healthy and productive economy. In the decades after World War II, when the United States was the only developed country not devastated by wartime destruction, this country had the world's best infrastructure. Our electricity, gas, telecommunications, pipelines, and water utilities were mostly investor-owned. Our original superhighways were toll financed turnpikes in the Northeast and Midwest, soon followed by the nationwide Interstate highway system. Our airports developed revenue bond financing and became major facilities. Our investor-owned freight railroads struggled until deregulation in 1980 enabled them to begin to make a realistic return on their investments, and they invested their way to becoming the best in the world. Our seaports did reasonably well, with revenue-bond financing much like that of airports.

Today, in the second decade of the 21st century, U.S. infrastructure no longer compares so well. Many of our largest airports suffer from chronic congestion and some still lack world-class passenger amenities. Our air traffic control system no longer sets the pace for advanced technology and streamlined procedures—and is struggling to fund what it now estimates as a $42 billion NextGen modernization program. Our Interstate highway system is nearing the end of its original design life and lacks capacity in numerous key trucking corridors, while urban expressways suffer chronic congestion in the larger metro areas. Ports compete for limited—and agonizingly slow to be approved—federal dredging projects in hopes of remaining competitive after the Panama Canal expansion. And our inland waterways are plagued by aging and undersized locks that constrain the flow of bulk shipping.

One key benefit from a more robust embrace of PPP approaches would be *increased investment* in upgrading existing transportation infrastructure and adding needed capacity in strategic locations. But as I see it, an even more important benefit of greater use of the market mechanisms that are part of the PPP approach is *more-productive* infrastructure investments. I distrust huge totals of alleged infrastructure needs that are compiled by organizations whose members hope to design and build more projects. For the most part, those totals do not necessarily represent projects that meet a genuine market test—such as having a positive return on the investment it would take to build them. A project finance approach subjects proposed projects to a critically important test: will the project generate enough revenues to pay for itself, making it worthwhile for infrastructure funds to invest equity and for bond buyers to purchase the revenue bonds?

Another benefit of the PPP approach—and I'm speaking here about long-term concessions to either rebuild and modernize a facility or to build an entirely new one—

is to minimize the risk to taxpayers. Risk transfer is one of the major benefits of the PPP approach to transportation megaprojects. Megaprojects such as Boston's Big Dig or the Los Angeles Red Line Subway have a terrible track record of cost overruns, late completion, and significant traffic and revenue shortfalls. A global database of 258 highway and rail megaprojects in 20 countries found that 90% experienced cost overruns, with rail projects on average costing 45% more than estimated and highways costing 20% more. Most rail projects also had ridership shortfalls, averaging 39%. A properly structured long-term concession transfers cost-overrun risk, late-completion risk, and traffic and revenue risk from the government (i.e., the taxpayers) to the concession company, which has strong incentives to build the project within the budget, get it completed on time, and properly maintain it so it will attract and keep customers. Modernizing US transportation infrastructure will involve a very large number of megaprojects, costing upwards of several trillion dollars over the next several decades. So it is critically important to do this in ways that minimize risks to taxpayers.

An additional benefit of the long-term PPP approach is *guaranteed maintenance.* Deferred maintenance is a significant problem in much of our transportation infrastructure—bridges, some highways, and especially waterways. Our institutions seem to be more focused on building new things than on properly maintaining what we have already built. But the long-term PPP concession creates a quasi-owner of the facility for the duration of the concession agreement, and that entity has every incentive to keep the facility well-maintained so that it continues to attract paying customers. Moreover, maintenance standards are generally included in the long-term agreement, and can be enforced via financial penalties. So you can think of an infrastructure facility that has been modernized via a long-term concession as having the equivalent of a maintenance endowment built in.

UNDERLYING PROBLEMS WITH THE U.S. INFRASTRUCTURE FUNDING MODEL

The federal government's 20th-century model of funding transportation infrastructure relied on a combination of user taxes and general revenues, with the user taxes accounted for in four trust funds: Airports & Airways, Highways, Harbor Maintenance, and Inland Waterways. But that system is breaking down, for several reasons.

First, the user taxes are widely portrayed and perceived as just "taxes," and any increase is criticized as a "tax increase." By contrast, when electric bills go up to pay for increased energy costs or a new power plant, people may grumble but they understand that the electric company has to pay the costs of producing and delivering the electricity they want, need, and use.

Second, each of the above trust fund programs builds in significant redistribution from one user group to another and from one region to another, which is not only economically inefficient but also generates political disaffection (and resistance to user tax increases).

Third, over time Congress has added numerous unfunded mandates (such as Buy America and Davis-Bacon) to federal transportation dollars, which increases the cost of building things with federal money and leads to further disaffection with the program.

Fourth, since most federal grant money is for new capacity, the lure of that money (despite its added cost) tends to bias state and local spending decisions toward new construction at the expense, in some cases, of maintenance.

The fifth and most important drawback of the current federal approach, in my view, is that by making annual capital spending money available, it encourages state and local governments to fund large capital projects out of annual appropriations *rather than financing* such long-lived assets. A basic principle of public finance is that long-lived assets should be financed, so that their benefits become available in the near term and are paid for by their users over the useful life of the asset, while the users enjoy the benefits of the improved facility. This is, of course, how the majority of people pay for their housing. But it is also how electric, gas, and water utilities pay for their capital projects, as well as railroads, toll roads, air traffic control providers overseas, and, to a considerable extent, U.S. airports and seaports (despite their also receiving some federal support from their respective trust funds).

With the ongoing federal government fiscal crisis, general fund money to supplement and subsidize the transportation trust funds will become an undependable and unsustainable funding source for transportation infrastructure. So it is time to fundamentally rethink how we fund and manage U.S. transportation infrastructure.

RETHINKING INFRASTRUCTURE, SECTOR BY SECTOR

Retooling the federal government's role in transportation infrastructure should begin with the principles of federalism. One major reason why federal transportation funds don't go far enough is that they are spread too thin, trying to do too many things. This is especially the case for the Highway Trust Fund, which originated as the means to pay for creating a nationwide superhighway network and has gradually evolved into an all-purpose transportation public works program. So the first principle should be: figure out what is truly federal and devolve state-level concerns to the states and urban/regional concerns to cities and counties.

The second principle is to shift as much as possible from funding to *financing*. That means two related things. First, shift from federal grants to federal loans. And shift from user taxes paid to the US Treasury to user fees paid to the actual infrastructure provider.

And the third principle is to give states and local governments tools to do more, such as reducing unfunded mandates and removing federal obstacles to increased use of long-term PPPs. One way to do that would be to remove entirely any difference in the tax treatment of bonds, whether for government infrastructure or PPP infrastructure.

In a January 2013 Reason Foundation policy brief, I sketched out how these principles might apply to the major categories of federally supported transportation infrastructure. A brief summary is as follows.

Airports

U.S. commercial airports are already largely user-funded, with revenues from airlines (landing charges and space rentals), passengers (passenger facility charges), and service providers (car rental firms, parking, shops and restaurants) paying for operating costs and debt service on airport bonds. Federal Airport Improvement Program (AIP) grants are a relatively small portion of airport budgets at large and medium hubs. As far back as 1987, a US DOT study demonstrated that large, medium, small, and non-hub commercial airports could replace their AIP funds with PFCs, and that could be done today. Self-supporting airports need not be privatized, but those seeking better management and lower-risk megaproject improvements should have the freedom to opt for privatization, as their counterparts in the rest of the developed world already do.

A separate question is whether there should be a continued federal role in funding non-commercial airports. Small towns that have a general aviation airport have some degree of competitive advantage as a place to live and do business compared with those that don't. That argument would support local funding as a choice to be made by such communities. The politics of this question at the federal level may be daunting, but this is exactly the kind of issue the entire federal budget needs to confront in rethinking what functions are truly federal and which are more appropriately left to state and local levels of government.

Air traffic control

Nearly all developed countries have de-politicized their ATC providers by converting them into self-supporting air navigation service providers, regulated at arm's length by the national aviation safety regulator. This course has been recommended repeatedly by think tanks, the US DOT in 1994, and the Mineta Commission in 1997. This kind of reform is now being talked about by aviation stakeholders concerned over the FAA's poor track record in modernizing the system and the uncertain future of federal aviation funding. Creating a U.S. equivalent of the nonprofit, user-governed Nav Canada would be a good solution, and is likely to be the best way to ensure that the portions of the NextGen modernization that actually provide user benefits exceeding their costs get implemented. With its own revenue stream paid by aircraft operators, the corporation could issue investment-grade revenue bonds to fund modernization investments, and the governing board of aviation stakeholders would vet the plans to be sure their user benefits exceeded their cost.

Highways and Bridges

Sorting out responsibilities among levels of government would have the federal government responsible for a national network of limited-access superhighways (the 21st century version of the Interstates), states responsible for most other highways, and metro areas responsible for their streets and roads. With fuel taxes as a declining revenue source over the coming decades, states (as the largest owner of highways) would take the lead in phasing in mileage-based user fees for state and local roads to replace fuel taxes. For the limited access system, tolling and PPPs would facilitate reconstruction and modernization of the existing Interstates, urban expressways, and portions of the National Highway System that should be upgraded to Interstate status. Given the likely ability of toll finance to handle most of the cost of Interstate reconstruction and modernization, the federal government's funding role would likely shift from grants to loans, primarily for states where traffic volume was insufficient to generate enough toll revenue. The federal role would also be important for ensuring nationwide inter-operability of all-electronic tolling on the limited-access system and mileage-based user fees on state and local roads.

Urban transit is an inherently local function of government, despite its being included in the Highway Trust Fund since the early 1980s. This issue is analogous to small general aviation airports—obviously good things for communities to have, but not obviously federal in nature. The politics of devolving this are also analogous to those of small airports, but are again part of the overall challenge of rethinking the role of the federal government in our multi-tiered governmental structure.

Seaports

Like airports, seaports are largely user-funded and bond-financed today. The Harbor Maintenance Tax is unnecessary, and instead of being reformed so that all the dollars collected each year are spent on port projects, it should be abolished, for several reasons. First, all ports are inherently in competition with other ports, so there are local benefits but not national benefits from the improvements funded by this trust fund. Second, the Corps of Engineers' feasibility studies can take over a decade, which generally delays needed projects which could proceed much sooner if judged bondable by the capital markets. Third, there is a long history of critical assessment of the objectivity of Corps feasibility studies, which provide a much less reliable guide to sound investment than the capital markets. Fourth, the tax is based on a percentage of the value of the cargo, not the draft of the ship (which is the relevant measure for assessing benefits of the dredging projects the tax ends up funding). This tax and trust fund are counterproductive to a sound US ports industry, overcharging some ships and undercharging others, cross-subsidizing ports that need dredging with money taken from ports that don't, and favoring some ports at the expense of their competitors. No national interest is served by continuing this program.

Waterways

Unlike ports, waterways are inherently interstate in nature, so it is not surprising that federal jurisdiction over inland waterways was established in the 19th century, based on the interstate commerce clause of the Constitution. However, because the federal government has responsibility does not mean that the current federal funding system makes sense or is sustainable. That system requires commercial users to pay just 8% of the annual cost of operating, maintaining, and improving the inland waterways system. The token tax on diesel fuel paid by those carriers is almost insignificant, and the heavily subsidized barge industry's reform proposals, though calling for an increase in that user tax, would put an even larger share of waterways costs on the general taxpayer. This is not merely unsustainable going forward; it is also grossly unfair to other modes that compete with barge lines, primarily railroads and, to a limited extent, trucks. Railroads pay 100% of the capital and operating cost of their infrastructure, while heavy trucks pay a large fraction of theirs, according to DOT cost responsibility studies.

In the last year or so, a few shipper groups and the Army Corps' own Institute for Water Resources have begun to discuss ways of tapping the capital markets to finance replacement of obsolete and undersized locks and dams. PPP concessions, of course, would require a bondable revenue stream, such as tolls to use modernized/replaced locks, as on the Panama Canal. In addition, repealing the Jones Act would permit barge operators to buy less-costly vessels, thereby offsetting part of the cost of increased user fees. In addition, since the inland waterways system is so extensive and the need to replace obsolete facilities is so large, consideration should be given to using long-term PPP concessions to modernize individual waterway segments, as France is beginning to do. Several Senators introduced legislation in March of this year to create a pilot program along these lines.

NEEDED POLICY CHANGES

What I have laid out in this testimony is an overview of how the federal role in transportation infrastructure could be rethought to better fit with the fiscal realities confronting the federal government in the decades ahead. Business as usual is simply not a sustainable option. This agenda could not be implemented overnight, but unless these ideas begin to be discussed seriously, our vitally important transportation infrastructure will continue to be short of investment capital, make sub-optimal investments with the capital it has, and create artificial winners and losers via cross-subsidies.

The key reform principles are (1) to sort out what functions are properly federal, state and local, (2) switch from funding to financing large capital improvements in infrastructure, (3) shift from user taxes paid to government to user fees paid directly to infrastructure providers, (4) empower all levels of government to make use of long-term PPP concessions, and (5) remove federal regulatory and tax obstacles to states and local governments taking on more infrastructure responsibilities.

Near-term federal regulatory and tax changes should include the following:

- Remove the federal cap on airport passenger facility charges (PFCs) and phase out AIP grants for commercial airports, reducing aviation excise tax rates accordingly.
- Remove the 10-airport limit on participating in the FAA's Airport Privatization Pilot Program.
- Remove the $15 billion cap on tax-exempt Private Activity Bonds for surface transportation PPP projects.
- Authorize states to implement all-electronic tolling on Interstate highways for the specific purpose of reconstructing and modernizing those highways.
- Return the maximum size of TIFIA loans to 33% of project budgets (rather than MAP-21's 49%), consistent with TIFIA's role as provider of gap, rather than primary, financing.
- Add TIFIA-like taxpayer protections to all other federal infrastructure credit programs, such as the Railroad Rehabilitation and Improvement Financing (RRIF) program to (a) limit loan amounts to 33% of total project cost, (b) require a dedicated revenue source for such projects, and (c) require an investment-grade rating on the project's primary financing.
- Eliminate the alternative minimum tax (AMT) on all PABs used for transportation infrastructure.
- Exempt harbor and waterway dredging projects from the Jones Act.
- Exempt highway and transit projects from the Davis-Bacon Act and Buy America Act.

Medium-term changes are mostly structural and organizational in nature, and should include the following:

- Separate the Air Traffic Organization (ATO) from the FAA, corporatize the ATO, and enable it to create its own bondable revenue stream from fees paid by aircraft operators; reduce aviation excise taxes accordingly.
- Eliminate the Harbor Maintenance Tax and wind down the Harbor Maintenance Trust Fund, allowing ports to be self-supporting.
- Refocus the Highway Trust Fund on interstate commerce, devolving its other responsibilities to state and local governments.
- Significantly increase user tax on diesel fuel on commercial inland waterway operators, as a step toward making the federal waterways program self-supporting.
- Authorize the Army Corps of Engineers to enter into long-term PPP agreements to rehabilitate and replace lock and dam facilities, financed by tolls on the new and refurbished facilities.

This is an ambitious agenda, affecting just a small part of the federal government's operations. But the status-quo federal role in transportation infrastructure is unsustainable. As part of putting the federal government's fiscal house in order, while ensuring robust and productive transportation infrastructure, rethinking the federal role along these lines is essential.

This concludes my testimony. I would be happy to answer questions or provide further details on any of the points I have made here.

———

PREPARED STATEMENT OF ROBERT PUENTES, SENIOR FELLOW AND DIRECTOR, METROPOLITAN INFRASTRUCTURE INITIATIVE, BROOKINGS INSTITUTION METROPOLITAN POLICY PROGRAM

Good morning Vice Chair Klobuchar and Members of the Committee. I very much appreciate the invitation to appear before you today. The purpose of my testimony is to discuss ways the federal government can engage in new partnerships with public and private investors to investment in infrastructure and, by so doing, put Americans back to work and rebalance the economy.

Of course, our challenge today is that the nation's economic recession and tense new focus on austerity means public resources for infrastructure are strained. As financial markets have contracted, all actors are suffering under tightened credit supplies. While state and local balance sheets are improving, overstretched budgets have led to a larger gap between infrastructure costs and revenues. As a result, meeting the nation's great needs for financing infrastructure requires an "all of the above" strategy.

Today, record low interest rates, coupled with attention from private firms and foreign funds, present growing opportunities for pragmatic public- and private-sector leaders to collaborate and innovate around infrastructure investments at the metropolitan scale, which can motivate state and federal officials to support these efforts. Indeed, leaders in many metros are already driving the development of new and innovative ways to deliver economically important infrastructure projects.

Modern freight and logistics projects in Los Angeles and Miami, state-of-the-art transit investments in Denver and Salt Lake City, advanced stormwater treatment upgrades in Washington and Philadelphia, broadband installations in Kansas City and Chattanooga are emblematic of the growing role states and cities are taking to build the infrastructure that will both support and enable the next American economy.

And so an enormous opportunity exists for Washington to adopt a fresh set of focused initiatives that can drive the nation toward economic renewal and support regional and state empowerment.

REVIVE BUILD AMERICA BONDS TO SUPPORT STATE AND LOCAL INVESTMENTS

Congress created the Build America Bonds (BABs) program in response to the Great Recession's dramatic effect on state, local, and other public entities' ability to issue debt. According to the U.S. Treasury, this credit crunch eventually led to a 68 percent drop in monthly municipal bond issuances and a doubling of borrowing costs.[1] Established through the American Recovery and Reinvestment Act (ARRA) of 2009, the two-year program authorized state and local governments to issue special taxable bonds that received either a 35 percent direct federal subsidy to the borrower (Direct Payment BABs) or a federal tax credit worth 35 percent of the interest owed to the investors (Tax-Credit BABs).

By harnessing the efficiencies of the taxable debt market, this unique structure decreased average borrowing costs for states and localities by 54 to 84 basis points compared to standard municipal bonds.[2] These lower costs, in turn, allowed borrowers to save an estimated $20 billion. The taxable nature of the bonds also incentivized a much broader group of investors to participate in the program, including pension funds and institutional investors. This expanded the traditional infrastructure investment base beyond the $2.8 trillion market for tax-exempt municipal bonds and made BABs appealing alternatives in the $30 trillion taxable bond market.

BABs proved wildly popular. From 2009 through the program's expiration in 2010, BABs financed one-third of all new state and local long-term debt issuances. In total, more than 2,275 separate bonds were issued to finance $182 billion in new infrastructure investment, driven by participation by all 50 states, Washington, DC, and two territories.[3] The greatest share of BAB funding (30 percent) went toward educational facilities. Water/sewer projects (13.8 percent), road/bridge projects (13.7 percent), and transit projects (8.7 percent) accounted for the next highest totals.[4] The use of BABs accelerated many of these major projects, which not only tended to have longer maturities, but also had a $6.2 million higher issuance value on average than tax-exempt municipal bonds.[5]

Despite initial skepticism, the BABs program successfully spurred investment in job intensive and economically important infrastructure projects across the country, while also stabilizing the municipal bond market. Importantly, it proved that bond issuers and investors were extremely receptive to the tax-credit and subsidy model.[6] Concerns about high origination costs for these unique structures also proved to be a minor issue, as prices fell drastically over the life of the program.

Recently, Congressional budget sequestration put a damper on the market as across-the-board spending cuts reduced the federal BABs subsidy by 8.7 percent.

[1] U.S. Department of the Treasury, "Analysis of Build America Bond Issuance and Savings," 2011.

[2] U.S. Department of the Treasury and Council of Economic Advisors, "A New Economic Analysis of Infrastructure Investment," 2012.

[3] U.S. Congress, Joint Committee on Taxation and the U.S. Department of the Treasury, "The Federal Revenue Effects of Tax-Exempt and Direct-Pay Credit Bond Provisions," 2011.

[4] Robert Puentes and Istrate, Emilia, "Whither Go the BABs?" The New Republic, 2010.

[5] Andrew Ang and others, "Build America Bonds," Cambridge: National Bureau of Economic Research, 2010.

[6] Lily Batchelder and others, "Efficiency and Tax Incentives: The Case for Refundable Tax Credits," Stanford Law Review 59 (23) 2006.

Smaller localities, in particular, now face pressure to call their BABs for a full redemption to cut costs and to take advantage of historically low interest rates in the municipal bond market. Some large BABs have been called as well, including a nearly $500 million refinancing in Columbus, Ohio.

However, long maturities, large issuances, and contractual provisions against par-value calls, are likely to limit the number of BAB redemptions. Even in the face of these challenges, BABs still outperform both treasuries and tax-exempt municipal bonds in U.S. markets.

Relative to the cost-savings for borrowers, the costs of administering a BABs program are quite low for the federal government. Based on initial government estimates, the annual cost of subsidizing the program under ARRA was approximately $340 million. Since the bonds were taxable, the government also expected to recoup some of these costs through the additional tax revenue produced. More recent estimates from the Joint Committee on Taxation put the annual net cost of a new BABs program at under $100 million.

The U.S. Treasury, furthermore, has indicated that lowering the tax subsidy from 35 to 28 percent would make the program revenue neutral "relative to the estimated future federal tax expenditure for tax-exempt bonds."[7] States and municipalities do not need the same aggressive subsidy they did after the 2008 financial crisis when borrowing costs spiked and the monthly issuance of bonds dropped by nearly one-third. It is important to note, however, that a significant drop in maturities would probably accompany the lower subsidy rate. At the same time, the true costs of the program to the federal government would not be known with complete precision, given the need to measure the amount of revenue currently being collected from tax-exempt debt.

EXEMPT PRIVATE ACTIVITY BONDS FROM THE ALTERNATIVE MINIMUM TAX

While municipal bonds are geared toward infrastructure projects with a public benefit, Private Activity Bonds (PABs) are directed at those projects that primarily benefit private entities but also serve some public purpose. PABs are issued by state and local governments for projects where more than 10 percent of the proceeds benefit a nongovernmental entity and are directly or indirectly paid back by a private business. In many cases, PABs are not tax-exempt and mainly cover privately owned and operated facilities. Depending on the specific project, however, there are a range of qualified private activities that can be financed by tax-exempt PABs, including sewage facilities and high-speed intercity rail facilities.

Federal tax policy, however, has undercut the potential of PABs to pull sorely needed private financing into critical infrastructure projects. The Alternative Minimum Tax (AMT), in particular, has limited their ability to attract potential investors over time. As a tax on individuals and corporations, the AMT is enforced beyond the regular income tax and takes into account the taxpayers' alternative minimum taxable income, which includes interest earned on PABs. PABs are also not necessarily tax-exempt for certain airport facilities and are further burdened by the AMT.

Lacking an AMT exemption, then, PABs hold less appeal for investors in many cases, thereby driving down demand for future investment and hindering the development of new infrastructure. State and local governments, as a result, must pay higher interest rates on PABs—more than 25 basis points on average compared to other tax-exempt bonds—to compensate investors for their tax liability, which in turn leads to higher infrastructure costs.[8]

To address these challenges, ARRA included provisions that exempted new PABs from the AMT in 2009 and 2010 and allowed refinancing of PABs issued from 2004 to 2008, which has helped promote increased infrastructure investment. Still, if private investors are continually dissuaded from PABs as a result of the AMT, necessary infrastructure upgrades may be delayed or put off altogether. Without the proper incentives in place, as they appeared under ARRA, project delivery will remain slow, innovation will be stifled, and users will be subjected to rapidly outdated and increasingly inefficient facilities. Ongoing financial and regulatory uncertainty, moreover, will continue to impede the competitiveness of metropolitan areas.

Based on estimates from the Joint Committee on Taxation, eliminating the AMT on all PABs (including airports) could potentially cost the government about $49

---

[7] U.S. Department of the Treasury, 2011.

[8] Government Finance Officers Association, "Issue Brief: AMT and Tax-Exempt Bonds," Washington, 2010.

million annually from 2012 to 2017.[9] At the same time, the exemption would generate billions of dollars in additional economic activity and lead to cost savings of almost $748 million for airports alone over the next ten years. Policymakers should be encouraged by these factors when considering a possible AMT exemption.

PABs play a large role in financing infrastructure projects across the country. Although many PABs are subject to a statewide volume cap (which creates a ceiling on the aggregate amount of qualified tax-exempt PABs that can be used in states each year), they help promote several short-term and long-term projects annually, ranging from highways to freight transfer facilities. Roughly $15 billion of qualified tax-exempt PABs have been issued annually in each of the past two years, with a notable increase following the AMT exemption in 2009. For example, the number of qualified tax-exempt PABs issued in 2010 marked the first increase in over three years. In contrast, when the exemption expired in 2011, the number of qualified tax-exempt PABs issued saw a marked decline (13 percent) across these projects nationwide.[10]

While some may emphasize the cost of an AMT exemption for PABs, the return on such an exemption far outweighs the expenditure. By making PABs more attractive to private investors, an AMT exemption can promote private and public sector involvement, which helps draw from a larger pool of investors and spread the financial risk involved in projects. This increased investment can consequently drive the construction of new infrastructure, improve public safety, fuel economic output, and create numerous jobs in the short and long term—all of which have stood as clear benefits in different proposals.

ESTABLISH A NATIONAL PPP UNIT TO SUPPORT BOTTOM-UP INFRASTRUCTURE INVESTMENT

Leveraging private financial resources and expertise to design, build, operate, maintain, and/or finance infrastructure has growing appeal. Whether repairing, upgrading, or augmenting an existing asset or constructing new infrastructure, the intent is to improve project delivery, and better share responsibilities and costs between the public and private sectors. The evidence from other countries—including some with less friendly business environments than in the U.S.—shows that these arrangements, if designed and implemented correctly, have the potential to improve on infrastructure delivery.

However, public/private partnerships (PPPs) are complicated contractual arrangements that can vary widely from project to project and from place to place. As the challenges to infrastructure development throughout the U.S. become more complex, there is a constant concern that public entities in some states, cities, and metropolitan areas are ill equipped to consider such deals and fully protect the public interest.

The U.S. Government Accountability Office recently noted that while the U.S. has done much to promote the benefits of PPPs, it needs to do more to assist states and metro areas in thinking through potential costs and trade-offs, as well as assessing national interests.[11]

A possible solution is the creation of a specialized institutional entity to assist with the expanding opportunities for PPPs. These so-called "PPP units" fulfill a variety of functions, including quality control, policy formulation and coordination, technical advice, standardization and dissemination, and promotion of PPPs.

Creating a federal PPP unit would provide states, cities, and metropolitan actors with the support and technical assistance needed from the procurement stage through long-term management of the projects by helping public actors determine the best Value for Money investment, assess long-term economic benefits of projects, and increase capacity to deal with contract changes over the life of the PPP. It would also create a more attractive, open, and robust environment that encourages private investment by creating predictability in the procurement process and demonstrating that the government actors involved want to "do business."

Looking around the world, PPP units are often located in a central government ministry (such as the Treasury Department) or in a line ministry that is closely related to infrastructure policy (such as the Department of Transportation). In the

[9] U.S. Department of Transportation, "Final Report: The Future of Aviation Advisory Committee," 2011.

[10] Council of Development Finance Agencies, "2011 National Volume Cap Report," Columbus, 2012.

[11] U.S. Government Accountability Office, "Highway Public-Private Partnerships: More Rigorous Up-front Analysis Could Better Secure Potential Benefits and Protect the Public Interest," GAO–08–44, 2008.

U.S., the Office of Management and Budget (OMB) is the most appropriate agency to house a PPP unit.[12]

Budget costs for a federal PPP Unit should be no more that $3 million annually. The PPP unit will be roughly the size of the Council on Environmental Quality (CEQ), located within the Executive Office of the President, which has a similar annual budget that covers support and administrative staff, as well as salaries and office and communications expenses.

There is no one-size-fits-all design of a PPP unit, but U.S. public entities could learn from experiences of other countries and from the growing track record in several U.S. states. A PPP unit reflects not only the needs of a particular PPP program, but also the administrative capacity and political structure of a specific government. Ultimately, the success of an American PPP unit will depend on a clear and consistent national plan and strategy for infrastructure development.

CREATE A REPATRIATION TAX HOLIDAY TO CAPITALIZE A NATIONAL INFRASTRUCTURE BANK

Another way to provide technical assistance and expertise to states and other public entities that cannot develop internal capacity to deal with the projects themselves is through the creation of a national infrastructure bank (NIB).

If designed and implemented appropriately, an NIB has the potential to leverage billions of dollars of private investment in important projects across the country. An NIB can not only provide a streamlined selection process for projects, but also apply a more rigorous standard for evaluating critical investments in energy, transportation, water, telecommunications, and other infrastructure assets attractive to private investors. Beyond bridges, roads, and other conventional projects, the NIB could spur cutting-edge investments in clean technologies, efficient energy distribution, and new resilient infrastructure assets.

The establishment of an NIB will send a strong signal to the private sector: the federal government is committed and open to private involvement in infrastructure financing and delivery. Today, private-sector financiers and investors are understandably frustrated with the lack of clarity concerning the rules of engagement when working with the federal government. This confusion hinders the development of robust public-private partnership markets in many states and localities.

Among the possible ways to capitalize an NIB, a one-time repatriation tax holiday could be used to unlock billions of dollars of domestically untaxed capital to fund the creation of a national infrastructure bank. In total, American corporations hold over $1.5 trillion in domestically untaxed deferred dividend payments that are routed through foreign countries including Ireland, the Netherlands, the Cayman Islands, Barbados, and other so-called "tax-havens." Because of the complexity and risk of these tax structures, the majority of firms that take advantage of these shelters are large and well-established corporations.

While a similar repatriation holiday created through the 2004 American Jobs Creation Act failed to generate significant domestic stimulus, a targeted program focused on infrastructure has the potential to deliver job creating and economy building projects for decades to come.

By directing a percentage of the recovered taxes into the NIB or compelling corporations to invest a portion of the repatriated funds into a special class of bonds that supports this institution, Congress can encourage infrastructure investment in a time of political gridlock. Depending on the specific goals of the NIB, capitalizing it can occur in a flexible manner as well, with levels ranging from $10 billion to $50 billion.

Of course, there are real costs associated with any repatriation based program. Firm behavior after 2004, for instance, illustrated how a new repatriation holiday can reduce government revenues in following years. The Joint Committee on Taxation estimates that a one year seventy percent deduction on repatriated profits capped at $500 million per firm would cost the Treasury $41.7 billion over the next decade.[13]

The overall cost of the holiday is driven both by the direct loss of revenue on regularly repatriated funds that are taxed at standard rates, but also by the long-term consequences of corporate behavior change. A repatriation holiday may incentivize corporations to restructure their foreign subsidiaries to hold more funds overseas, and they may relocate workers to tax-haven countries, hoping to reap the benefits

---

[12] Emilia Istrate and Robert Puentes, "Moving Forward on Public Private Partnerships: U.S. and International Experience with PPP Units," Washington: Brookings Institution, 2011.

[13] U.S. Congress Joint Committee on Taxation, "Revenue Estimates for Two Dividends-Received Deductions Proposals," 2011.

of future tax breaks. Among other effects, the holiday can further complicate an already byzantine tax-code and increase horizontal tax inequality by giving special privileges to firms that chose to hold funds overseas, which in effect rewards tax-evading behavior. However, policymakers must also weigh the long- and short-term tax consequences of a repatriation holiday against the strategic and financial benefits of an NIB.

Madam Vice Chairman, in this era of fiscal constraint I firmly believe the federal government will need to optimize the workings of the emerging federal-state-metro order. The urgency and complexity of the challenges facing the nation today suggest the need to devise new ways to increase impact and do more with less. At every turn, then, Washington should consider how to enhance the performance of the coming wave of co-developed, bottom-up problem-solving and then how to scale it up.[14] Most of what I have described would require legislative action, possibly as part of a major tax reform bill or through budget negotiations. It won't be easy but the time is ripe to invest in infrastructure projects that put us on the path to a more productive and sustainable economy.

The views expressed in this testimony are those of the author alone and do not necessarily represent those of the staff, officers, or trustees of The Brookings Institution.

PREPARED STATEMENT OF CHRIS EDWARDS, DIRECTOR OF TAX POLICY STUDIES AND EDITOR OF *www.DownsizingGovernment.org*, Cato Institute

Mr. Chairman and members of the committee, thank you for inviting me to testify today. My comments will examine the federal role in infrastructure and discuss opportunities for greater private investment.

The importance of infrastructure investment for U.S. economic growth is widely appreciated. But policy discussions often get sidetracked by a debate regarding the level of federal spending. To spur growth, it is more important to ensure that investment is as efficient as possible and that investment responsibilities are optimally allocated between the federal government, the states, and the private sector.

Federal infrastructure spending often gets bogged down in mismanagement and cost overruns. And decades of experience show that many federal investments get misallocated to low-value activities because of politics. That's why we should tackle the nation's infrastructure challenges by decentralizing the financing, management, and ownership of investments as much as possible. State and local governments and the private sector are more likely to make sound investments without the federal subsidies and regulations that distort their decisionmaking.

My testimony will discuss the growing private sector involvement in financing, constructing, and operating infrastructure such as highways, bridges, and aviation facilities around the world. Privatization of infrastructure promises to improve economic efficiency, spur growth, and reduce financial burdens on governments and taxpayers. As such, policymakers should focus on removing federal barriers to privatization.

FEDERAL INFRASTRUCTURE IN PERSPECTIVE

Most of America's infrastructure is provided by the private sector, not governments. Indeed, private infrastructure spending—on factories, freight rail, pipelines, refineries, and other items—is much larger than federal, state, and local government infrastructure spending combined.

A broad measure of infrastructure spending is gross fixed investment, as measured in the national income accounts.[1] In 2012 private investment was $2 trillion, compared to federal, state, and local government investment of $472 billion. Excluding defense, government investment was $367 billion. Thus, private infrastructure investment in the United States is five times larger than total nondefense government investment.

One implication of the data is that if policymakers want to boost infrastructure spending, they should make policy reforms to spur private investment. Cutting the federal corporate income tax rate, for example, would increase the net returns to a broad range of private infrastructure, and thus spur greater investment.

Nonetheless, government infrastructure is certainly important to the economy. But I am skeptical of claims that the United States has an infrastructure crisis be-

---

[14] Bruce Katz and Mark Muro, "Remaking Federalism, Renewing the Economy: Resetting Federal Policy to Recharge the Economy, Stabilize the Budget, and Unleash State and Metropolitan Innovation," Washington: Brookings Institution, 2012.

[1] U.S. Bureau of Economic Analysis, National Income and Product Accounts, Table 1.5.5, *www.bea.gov*.

cause governments are not spending enough. For one thing, government investment as a share of gross domestic product (GDP) in the United States is in line with the other nations of the Organization for Economic Cooperation and Development (OECD). In 2010 government gross fixed investment in the United States was 3.5 percent of GDP, which was a little higher than the OECD average of 3.3 percent.[2]

Another reason for skepticism that governments are underinvesting is that some measures of infrastructure quality have shown steady improvement. For example, Federal Highway Administration (FHWA) data show that the nation's bridges have steadily improved in quality.[3] Of the roughly 600,000 bridges in the country, the share that are "structurally deficient" has fallen from 22 percent in 1992 to 11 percent in 2012, while the share that are "functionally obsolete" has fallen from 16 percent to 14 percent.

The surface quality of our interstate highways has also steadily improved. A study by Federal Reserve economists examining FHWA data found that "since the mid-1990s, our nation's interstate highways have become indisputably smoother and less deteriorated."[4] And the economists concluded that the interstate system is "in good shape relative to its past condition."

PROBLEMS WITH FEDERAL INFRASTRUCTURE SPENDING

There are frequent calls for increased federal spending on infrastructure, but advocates usually ignore the problems and failures of past federal efforts. There is a history of pork-barrel politics and bureaucratic mismanagement of many types of federal investment. Here are some of the problems:

- *Investment is misallocated.* Federal investments are often not based on actual marketplace demands. Amtrak investment, for example, has long been spread around to low-population areas where passenger rail makes little economic sense. Most of Amtrak's financial losses come from long-distance routes through rural areas that account for only a small fraction of all riders.[5] Every lawmaker wants an Amtrak route through their state, so investment gets misallocated away from where it is really needed, such as the Northeast corridor.
- *Investments are utilized inefficiently.* Government infrastructure is often utilized inefficiently because supply and demand are not balanced by market prices. The vast water infrastructure operated by the Bureau of Reclamation, for example, greatly underprices irrigation water in western United States. The result has been wasted resources, harm to the environment, and a looming water crisis in many areas in the West.[6]
- *Investment is mismanaged.* Federal agencies don't have the strong incentives that private businesses do to ensure that infrastructure projects are completed and operated efficiently. Federal highway, energy, airport, and air traffic control projects, for example, have often suffered large cost overruns.[7] The Big Dig in Boston—which was two-thirds funded by the federal government—exploded in cost to five times the original estimate.[8] U.S. and foreign studies have found that privately financed infrastructure projects are less likely to have cost overruns than traditional government projects.[9]
- *Mistakes are replicated across the nation.* Perhaps the biggest problem with federal intervention in infrastructure is that when Washington makes mistakes it replicates them across the nation. High-rise public housing projects, for example, were a terrible idea that federal funding helped spread nationwide. Federal subsidies for light-rail projects have biased cities to opt for these expensive sys-

[2] This is OECD data for government gross fixed capital spending. The data underlies Figure 2.1 in OECD, "Pension Funds Investment in Infrastructure: A Survey," September 2011.

[3] Federal Highway Administration data is available at *www.fhwa.dot.gov/bridge/deficient.cfm*.

[4] Jeffrey R. Campbell and Thomas N. Hubbard, "The State of Our Interstates," Federal Reserve Bank of Chicago, July 2009.

[5] Tad DeHaven, "Privatizing Amtrak," Cato Institute, June 2010, *www.downsizinggovernment.org/transportation/privatizing-amtrak*.

[6] Chris Edwards and Peter J. Hill, "Cutting the Bureau of Reclamation and Reforming Water Markets," Cato Institute, February 2012, *www.downsizinggovernment.org/interior/cutting-bureau-reclamation*.

[7] Chris Edwards, "Government Cost Overruns," Cato Institute, March 2009, *www.downsizinggovernment.org/government-cost-overruns*.

[8] For background, see the *Boston Globe*'s "Easy Pass" series of reports by Raphael Lewis and Sean Murphy, *www.boston.com/globe/metro/packages/bechtel*.

[9] For example, see Allen Consulting Group and the University of Melbourne, "Performance of PPPs and Traditional Procurement in Australia," November 30, 2007. And see Richard Kerrigan, "P3 Study: Over 80% of U.S. Highway P3s Were On-Time and On-Budget," *Public Works Financing*, November 2012, p. 16.

tems, even though they are generally less efficient and flexible than bus systems.[10] High-speed rail represents another federal effort to induce the states to spend money on uneconomical infrastructure.[11]

- *Burdensome Regulations.* A final problem with federal infrastructure spending is that it usually comes part and parcel with piles of regulations. Federal Davis-Bacon labor rules, for example, raise the cost of building state and local infrastructure. In general, federal regulations impose one-size-fits-all solutions on the states even though the states may have diverse infrastructure needs.

GLOBAL TREND TOWARD PRIVATIZATION

The answer to America's infrastructure challenges is not greater federal intervention, but greater involvement by the private sector. There has been a worldwide trend toward infrastructure privatization. Since 1990 about $900 billion of state-owned assets have been sold in OECD countries, about 63 percent of which has been infrastructure assets.[12] What spurred the trend? The OECD says that "public provision of infrastructure has sometimes failed to deliver efficient investment with misallocation across sectors, regions, or time, often due to political considerations. Constraints on public finance and recognized limitations on the public sector's effectiveness in managing projects have led to a reconsideration of the role of the state in infrastructure provision."[13]

Short of full privatization, many countries have partly privatized infrastructure through public-private partnerships ("PPPs" or "P3s"). P3s differ from traditional government contracting by shifting various elements of financing, management, operations, and project risks to the private sector. In a 2011 report, the OECD found a "widespread recognition" around the world of "the need for greater recourse to private sector finance" in infrastructure.[14]

Unfortunately, the United States "has lagged behind Australia and Europe in privatization of infrastructure such as roads, bridges and tunnels," notes the OECD.[15] About one fifth of public infrastructure spending in Britain is now through the P3 process, and in Canada P3s account for between 10 to 20 percent of public infrastructure spending.[16]

According to *Public Works Financing*, only 1 of the top 38 firms doing transportation P3s around the world are American.[17] Of more than 700 transportation projects listed in the newsletter, only 28 are in the United States. Canada—a country with one-tenth of our population—has about the same number of P3 deals as we do.

Nonetheless, a number of U.S. states have moved ahead with P3s and privatization. Some projects in Virginia illustrate the opportunities:[18]

- *Capital Beltway.* Transurban and Fluor have built and are now operating new toll lanes along 14 miles of I–495. The firms used debt and equity to finance most of the project's $2 billion cost.[19] The lanes were completed on time and on budget in 2012.
- *Dulles Greenway.* The Greenway is a privately owned toll highway in Northern Virginia completed in the mid-1990s with $350 million of private debt and equity.[20]
- *Jordan Bridge.* FIGG Engineering Group and partners financed and constructed a $142 million highway bridge over the Elizabeth River between Chesapeake and Portsmouth. The bridge opened in 2012, and its cost will be paid back to investors over time with toll revenues.[21]

---

[10] Randal O'Toole, "Urban Transit," Cato Institute, June 2010, *www.downsizinggovernment.org/transportation/urban-transit.*

[11] Randal O'Toole, "High-Speed Rail," Cato Institute, June, 2010, *www.downsizinggovernment.org/transportation/high-speed-rail.*

[12] Organization for Economic Cooperation and Development, "Pension Funds Investment in Infrastructure: A Survey," September 2011.

[13] Organization for Economic Cooperation and Development, "Pension Funds Investment in Infrastructure: A Survey," September 2011, p. 34.

[14] Organization for Economic Cooperation and Development, "Pension Funds Investment in Infrastructure: A Survey," September 2011, p. 27.

[15] Organization for Economic Cooperation and Development, "Pension Funds Investment in Infrastructure: A Survey," September 2011, p. 107.

[16] *Public Works Financing*, October 2011, p. 18, *www.pwfinance.net.*

[17] *Public Works Financing*, October 2011, p. 3, *www.pwfinance.net.*

[18] Details on Virginia's PPPs are available at *www.vappta.org/projects.asp.*

[19] *www.495expresslanes.com/project-background.*

[20] *http://dullesgreenway.com.*

[21] *www.figgbridge.com/jordan—bridge.html.*

There are many advantages of infrastructure P3s and privatization. Most fundamentally, when private businesses are taking the risks and putting their profits on the line, funding is more likely to get allocated to high-return projects and completed in the most efficient manner.

U.S. and foreign experience indicate that P3s are more likely to be completed on time and on budget than traditional government contracts. An Australian study compared 21 P3 (or PPP) projects with 33 traditional projects and found: "PPPs demonstrate clearly superior cost efficiency over traditional procurement . . . PPPs provide superior performance in both the cost and time dimensions, and ... the PPP advantage increases (in absolute terms) with the size and complexity of projects." [22] A government official overseeing the Capital Beltway P3 lauded the private firms in charge for their rapid and nonbureaucratic way of solving problems that arose during construction, which is "not the way government works typically," he said.[23]

The publisher of *Public Works Financing*, William Reinhardt, notes that "the design-build contracting approach used in a P3 guarantees the construction price and project completion schedule of large, complex infrastructure projects that often befuddle state and local governments, as was the case with Boston's Big Dig." [24] Reinhardt says that P3 projects typically experience capital cost savings of 15 to 20 percent compared to traditional government contracting.

A Brookings Institution study noted that the usual process of government investing decouples the construction from the future management of facilities, which results in contractors having little incentive to build projects that will minimize long-term costs.[25] P3s solve this problem because the same company both builds and operates new facilities. "Many advantages of PPP stem from the fact that they bundle construction, operations, and maintenance in a single contract. This provides incentives to minimize life-cycle costs," notes the study.

Another reason privatized infrastructure is efficient is that businesses can tap capital markets to build capacity and meet market demands, without having to rely on the instability of government budgeting. Our air traffic control (ATC) system, for example, needs major upgrades, but the Federal Aviation Administration (FAA) cannot count on a stable federal funding stream. The recent threatened disruptions to ATC from federal budget sequester cuts illustrate the hazards of having infrastructure depend on federal funding.

The solution in this case is to privatize the U.S. air traffic control system, as Canada did with its system in 1996 with very favorable results.[26] Canada's ATC is run by the nonprofit corporation Nav Canada separate from the government. It raises revenues from its customers to cover its operational and capital costs. Nav Canada is a "global leader in delivering top class performance," says the International Air Transport Association, which has given the company multiple awards.

HURDLES TO PRIVATE INFRASTRUCTURE INVESTMENT

Despite the benefits of private infrastructure investment, federal policies have long created hurdles for the states in pursuing privatization. Federal policymakers should free states from regulations and subsidies so that they can become "laboratories of democracy" for infrastructure. Here are some barriers to private infrastructure that policymakers should examine:

- *Tax exemption on municipal bond interest.* When state and local governments borrow funds to build infrastructure, the interest on the debt is tax-free under the federal income tax. That allows governments to finance infrastructure at a lower cost than private businesses, which stacks the deck against the private provision of infrastructure. Policymakers should consider phasing-out the tax exemption on state and local bond interest, perhaps in exchange for reducing overall tax rates on capital income.
- *Income and Property Taxation.* Government facilities don't pay income taxes. While state-owned airports are tax-exempt, for example, a for-profit airport

[22] Allen Consulting Group and the University of Melbourne, "Performance of PPPs and Traditional Procurement in Australia," November 30, 2007.

[23] Comments of Ron Kirby, Washington Council of Governments, Public Works Financing, December 2012, p. 21.

[24] William G. Reinhardt, "The Case For P3s in America," Public Works Financing, January 2012.

[25] Eduardo Engel, Ronald Fischer, and Alexander Galetovic, "Public-Private Partnerships to Revamp U.S. Infrastructure," Brookings Institution, February 2011.

[26] Chris Edwards and Robert W. Poole, Jr., "Airports and Air Traffic Control," Cato Institute, June 2010, *www.downsizinggovernment.org/transportation/airports-atc*. And see Chris Edwards, "Privatize the FAA!" Daily Caller, April 24, 2013.

would have its net earnings taxed at both the state and federal levels.[27] Similarly, government-owned facilities are exempt from property taxes almost everywhere in the United States, while for-profit businesses often bear a heavy burden of property taxes on their land, structures, and machinery and equipment.[28] Note that by privatizing infrastructure and thus subjecting it to taxation, governments would be broadening the tax base. They could use the added revenues from base broadening to reduce overall tax rates, which would spur greater investment of all types in the economy.

- *Crowding Out.* The existence of government infrastructure—which is often provided at artificially low prices to the public—deters potential private investments. Private highways, for example, face an uneven playing field because drivers on a private highway would have to pay the private tolls plus the gasoline taxes that fund the government's "free" highways.
- *Federal subsidies.* The crowding out problem is exacerbated when federal subsidies tilt state and local decisionmakers in favor of government provision. Potential private airports, for example, are not eligible for most federal airport subsidies. Or consider that before the 1960s most urban bus and rail services in America were privately owned and operated. But that ended with the passage of the Urban Mass Transportation Act of 1964. The Act provided subsidies only to government-owned bus and rail systems, not private systems.[29] That prompted state and local governments across the country to take over private systems, swiftly ending more than a century of private transit investment in America's cities.
- *Federal regulations.* Federal regulations have restricted efforts to privatize state and local infrastructure. One issue has been that states receiving federal aid for their facilities have been required to repay the aid if the facilities are privatized. These rules have been liberalized over the years, but they may still create a disincentive to privatize in some cases.[30] Another issue is that tolling has been generally prohibited on interstate highways, which prevented P3-style projects. However, the 2012 highway bill (MAP–21) allowed for the tolling of new capacity on the interstates, which is a step forward.[31] Federal policymakers should work to eliminate remaining regulations that stand in the way of infrastructure privatization.[32]
- *Labor Unions.* Privatization would undermine the power of the public-sector unions that often dominate government services, and so unions actively lobby against reforms. Unions lobby against contracting-out airport security screening operations.[33] The National Air Traffic Controllers Association lobbies against ATC privatization. And in the District of Columbia, unions are trying to block a proposal to allow private operation of some bus services.[34] One solution to the problem is to ban monopoly unions ("collective bargaining") in the public sector, which is the rule in a number of states.[35]
- *Social Security.* The structuring of Social Security as a pay-as-you-go system is a negative for privatized infrastructure. One of the fuels for the rise in P3s in other countries has been growing investment by pension funds. Infrastructure investment is a good fit for pension funds because it provides a return over a very long period of time, which matches the pattern of long-term liabilities of these funds. In Canada and Australia, the growth in P3s has been partly driven

---

[27] There appears to be just one private for-profit commercial airport in the United States. The Branson Airport in Branson, Missouri, opened in 2009. See *www.flybransom.com.*

[28] For background on the tax exemption on government land, see H. Woods Bowman, "Reexamining the Property Tax Exemption," Lincoln Institute of Land Policy, July 2003. For information on property tax payments by businesses, see Council on State Taxation and Ernst and Young, "Total State and Local Business Taxes," July 2012.

[29] National Research Council, "Contracting for Bus and Demand-Responsive Transit Services," Special Report 258, 2001, Chapter 2.

[30] President George H.W. Bush's 1992 Executive Order 12803 was designed to encourage federal approvals of state privatizations, and it liberalized the grant repayment requirements.

[31] Robert S. Kirk, "Tolling of Interstate Highways," Congressional Research Service, February 13, 2013.

[32] For a discussion of the regulatory barriers to privatizing airports, see National Academy of Sciences, Transportation Research Board, "Considering and Evaluating Airport Privatization," Airport Cooperative Research Program report no. 66, 2012, pp. 45–46. See also Jerry Ellig, The $7.7 Billion Mistake: Federal Barriers to State and Local Privatization, Joint Economic Committee Staff Report, February 1996.

[33] Joe Davidson, "Decision to Keep Federal Screeners at Calif. Airport Buoys Labor," Washington Post, January 10, 2013.

[34] Dana Hedgpeth, "Union Aims To Block D.C. Bus Plan," Washington Post, July 20, 2013.

[35] Chris Edwards, "Public-Sector Unions," Cato Institute Tax and Budget Bulletin no. 61, March 2010.

by the pools of savings created by reformed government retirement programs. In the United States, reforms to create Social Security private accounts would create a large pool of long-term savings to help fuel private infrastructure investment.

Policymakers should reduce the hurdles to private investment so that we can attract more entrepreneurs to tackle the nation's infrastructure challenges. After all, private infrastructure is not a new or untried idea. Urban transit services used to be virtually all private.[36] And before the 20th century, private turnpike companies in America built thousands of miles of toll roads.[37] The takeover of much infrastructure by governments in the 20th century was a mistake, and policymakers here and abroad are now working to correct the overreach.

In sum, there is widespread agreement that America should have top-notch infrastructure to spur growth and compete in the global economy. The way forward is for the federal government to cut subsidies and reduce its control over the nation's infrastructure. State and local governments should be encouraged to innovate with privatization and P3s to the fullest extent possible.

Thank you for holding these important hearings.

○

---

[36] Randal O'Toole, "Urban Transit," Cato Institute, June 2010, *www.downsizinggovernment.org/transportation/urban-transit.*
[37] Gabriel Roth, "Federal Highway Funding," Cato Institute, June 2010, *www.downsizinggovernment.org/transportation/highway-funding.*